But I want to be a
NURSE

Pilar De La Cruz Samoulian

Author's Tranquility Press
ATLANTA, GEORGIA

Copyright © 2024 by Pilar De La Cruz Samoulian

All rights reserved. No part of this publication may be reproduced, distributed or transmitted in any form or by any means, including photocopying, recording, or other electronic or mechanical methods, without the prior written permission of the publisher, except in the case of brief quotations embodied in critical reviews and certain other noncommercial uses permitted by copyright law. For permission requests, write to the publisher, addressed "Attention: Permissions Coordinator," at the address below.

Pilar De La Cruz Samoulian /Author's Tranquility Press
3900 N Commerce Dr. Suite 300 #1255
Atlanta, GA 30344, USA
www.authorstranquilitypress.com

Ordering Information:
Quantity sales. Special discounts are available on quantity purchases by corporations, associations, and others. For details, contact the "Special Sales Department" at the address above.

But I Want To Be A Nurse / Pilar De La Cruz Samoulian
Hardback: 978-1-965075-51-7
Paperback: 978-1-964810-86-7
eBook: 978-1-964810-07-2

To my two sons, Stephen and Jeffrey, whose love has been constant throughout the years and whose support I relied on over the years to get me through the difficult times.

Prologue

This is the story of a poor young Mexican girl who came from a large family and who, from a very young age, had a dream of escaping the hard work in the fields of the San Joaquin Valley and someday becoming a registered nurse. She shares the trials and tribulations she faced along with the many barriers placed in her way on the path to success. Coming from meager beginnings, she overcame verbal, physical, emotional, and even sexual abuse as she struggled to find her way. Holding on tight to her dream, she did not let anyone dissuade her from her goal. It is a true inspiration to anyone who has a dream of bettering their life and who believes that education, dedication, and commitment are the keys to helping one overcome whatever challenges life may bring.

CHAPTER 1

Growing Up

I was the firstborn of parents who were migrant workers. They would follow the crops and travel throughout the San Joaquin Valley working in the fields, picking whatever crop was in season in order to make a living. They would leave me with my grandparents as they toiled day in and day out, coming home to visit me only on weekends. During the week, I was in the care of my monolingual, Spanish-speaking grandparents who, together with my aunts, lived on a ten-acre ranch on a quiet country road in rural Fresno County, next to the Kings River.

They lived in an older house that was cold in the winter—heated only by a small wood heater—and hot in the summer, with only fans to help move the hot air. The house had no indoor bathroom, and bedpans and buckets were used, if needed, during the night. During the day, there were visits to the outhouse, which was dark, hot, and smelly. I would have to be lifted up to sit over the hole that allowed me to do my business and remember always wanting to get out of that small dark room as quickly as possible. Fear of spiders and worry about the possibility of being bitten by a spider that was hiding in there just waiting for me was a great concern.

Being the first grandchild, I received my share of spoiling by my grandparents and aunts. One of my aunts was older and walked with much difficulty, shuffling back and forth as she had been afflicted with polio as a child, but she was very loving and always fussed over me. She was my father's sister. My other three aunts were my father's stepsisters and were teenagers. The small amount of English I learned at an early age was learned from them. I also learned to love music because of them as they would listen to music on the radio and did a little dancing on the side. They were fun, energetic, and doted on me during the week. On the weekends my parents would come home and pick me up and take me to their house which was right next door.

Sometimes, I would sneak over to my grandparent's home and visit, especially whenever my grandmother and aunts would make rice pudding. I would literally stand on a chair next to the stove as my grandmother stirred the rice pudding, asking constantly if it was almost ready so we could eat it. The music would be playing, and I would be dancing on top of the chair to the music anxiously waiting to taste the rice pudding. Alas, my mother would find me and take me home. There would be tears shed as my mother would take me back home before the pudding was done. However, I knew that my aunts would always bring some over to me when it was ready.

My days consisted of playing with my doll and pretending to play house until being called into the house to eat. My grandfather had a milking cow which my aunts milked and brought the milk home for everyone to drink. During the spring, when the cows would eat the freshly grown green grass, the milk would have a terrible taste to it and was hard to drink due to the taste. My grandparents, trying to ensure good nutrition, would insist that I either drink my glass of milk or take a tonic which tasted even worse than the milk. However, my choice was always the tonic as it was only one tablespoon of the tonic as compared to one glass of the milk. To this day, milk is not a staple in my diet. Considering that I never drank much milk, it is surprising that my bone density results are always so positive. It must be all of the ice cream that I ate and have eaten over the years.

My grandparents were very devoted Catholics, and if my parents were not able to make it home on a weekend, I would go to church on Sunday with my aunts and grandparents. One of my aunts, who later became a nun, would take me by the hand and lead me to the very front row where we would sit for the entire mass. She must have figured that I would behave if we sat in the front. There were several church festivals such as the celebration for Our Lady of Guadalupe, where my grandmother would make a special dress for me and make me march in a parade dressed up as a *China Poblana*, in a traditional red-white-and-green dress, the colors of Mexico. I would dutifully put on my dress and walk in the parade alongside my aunts, singing and waving a flag. At the end of the parade, my tired body quickly fell asleep in the car on the way home.

On Sundays after mass, and on the way home, my aunts would nudge me to ask my grandfather if we could stop to get an ice cream cone at Foster Freeze. They knew that my grandfather would probably not ignore my request and sure enough, he would stop and buy me my *colita*, a vanilla ice cream cone. That made my weekend, and I was a happy camper all the way home. Upon our return home, my grandmother and aunts would cook a nice hearty meal, and we would all eat and then take a nap. During the hot summer months, we would walk to the river that ran next to the property and take a dip in the cool water; sometimes enjoying a picnic by the river.

At night, I would sleep with my aunts, and I remember them telling me stories as I fell asleep. Sometimes they would read to me, but mostly they told me stories. One of my favorites was the story of Peter Rabbit. I would ask them to tell it to me over and over again, in both English and Spanish.

Having lived with my grandparents and aunts for several years, I became very close to them and was sorry to leave their home when my parents built a small three-room home on another ranch and we moved there. Having turned four, preparations were being made for me to start kindergarten. The school that I would attend did not have a kindergarten class at the time, so my mother and another mother drove around the area talking to other parents about starting a kindergarten class at the school, and this was accomplished. As my birthday was in November, the school allowed me to start kindergarten early, at the age of four and-a half.

CHAPTER 2
Early School Years

The very first day of school was scary. I was taken to my kindergarten class by my mother, but because we lived in the country and my sister had been born, my mother made arrangements for me to take the bus home from school. Since it was not clear which bus to board, I just got on a bus not knowing whether or not it was the one that would pass by my house to drop me off. Never seeing my house, I stayed on the bus until it returned to the school; at which point, tears rolled down my face as I had not seen my home, so I just stayed on the bus. When the bus returned to the school, the bus driver noted that I was still sitting in my seat and asked why. Through my tears, I was able to tell him the reason. The principal of the school had to drive me home, but before he did, he instructed me on which bus to get on in the future. I never had any problems with the bus after that first day of school.

My English, on the other hand, was another problem. Having spoken mainly Spanish at home, my English was poor. I was made fun of by my classmates for not being able to say the words correctly. When wanting to say, "chair," I would instead say, "share." Not knowing how to say bathroom, the words used were *go pee pee*. However, being a quick learner, I was soon speaking with little to no accent and saying words correctly. I loved playing with all the different toys, especially the doll houses, got along well with the other children, and quickly made new friends. The comments by my teacher on my report card were always positive, and my parents were proud of my accomplishments. Practicing my English became very important to me, and my father, concerned that I might lose my Spanish would always make me tell him what

I had told him in English in Spanish. He would say, "You told me in English, now tell me in Spanish." It was a pain to have to repeat what I had just told him then, but now, I'm so happy he made me do that as I became bilingual, a very beneficial tool in today's world. Sometimes, when not remembering how to say something in Spanish, I would throw in some "Spanglish." My father hated this and would sternly say, "Either tell me in English or Spanish, but not both; and don't mix the languages!"

My parents were the typical Mexican parents. My father ruled the house with an iron fist; what he said went. My mother did as my father wanted and did not often question nor go against his wishes. My father worked very hard to keep a roof over our heads and make sure that we had food to eat. He bought dairy cows, and we had to milk them twice a day—early in the morning and at night. I hated milking the cows, and we were always rushing to make sure we had the milk tanks ready for the milk truck to pick up the milk before we got ready for school. My mother used the cream from the milk to make cheese and would sell it to make a little money on the side. I hated to hear the cows start mooing in the morning as that meant it was time to get up and milk them before getting ready for school. Shouts of joy could be heard when my father finally sold all of the cows in order to pay for my mother's ear surgery as we did not have any insurance at the time. However, having the cows meant that we always had meat in the house, as my father would slaughter a young cow and take it to the food locker to have the meat packaged.

My family consisted of my parents, myself, my sister Esther, my brother Jesse, my sister Terri, my baby sister Mattie, and my baby brother Eddie. There was seventeen years between myself and my baby brother. One day, I asked my mother why she did not have us closer together as there were three and four years between each child, and there seemed to be a divide between the older three and the youngest three. She quickly informed me that when I grew up, got married, and had my own children, I could have them as close in age as desired. However, even with the age difference, we grew up very close to one another. As the oldest, I was held responsible and would sometimes get in trouble when one of the younger ones misbehaved. I tried to set a good example for all of them and sometimes had to cover for them in order to save them from my father's wrath.

My mother was a very kind soul but was rather passive and had a hard time voicing her opinion or standing up for herself. She was a very religious person and made sure that we followed our faith. As an example, each year during holy week, the week before Easter, she would not let us watch any television. The only time the television was on during that week was when my father was watching the evening news, and there could be no talking or noisemaking while he was watching the news. Maybe that is the reason that I like to watch the nightly news.

My mother was the type of person who would always serve my father first, run his bath water, lay out his clothes for church or any special event, iron sheets and pillowcases and always made tortillas for breakfast, lunch, and dinner. When we would all work together on the ranch, we would come home to eat lunch, and my sisters and I would help her prepare the lunch. My father was always served first and was eating as we were still cooking the tortillas. When we were finally able to sit down to eat, he was finished eating and was ready to go back to work. Thus, we had to learn to eat fast if we wanted to eat. Sometimes coworkers and friends will ask why I eat so fast, and my response is that the habit of eating fast has still not been broken even after many decades.

The major holidays were very much like a regular day. We would have to work at least part of the day and then we would come home and cook the meal. On Christmas Eve, we would work in the field half the day and then come home and have to make the traditional tamales. My father would buy fifty to sixty pounds of *masa* (cornmeal) and mix the *masa* with lard to make it smooth for spreading. After he did that, his job was done, and we would have to spread the *masa* on the cornhusks. With so much *masa* to spread and getting a late start, sometimes we would often be up until after midnight finishing up making the tamales while my father was sound asleep. The next morning, we would have to get up early to go to church.

My dad's friends always seemed to find their way to our house on Christmas Eve as they knew we would be making tamales, and they always left with at least a dozen tamales.

We were quite poor, and we did not have many gifts to open on Christmas morning. Usually, if we received a gift for Christmas, it would be a pair of pajamas that we each needed. After seeing them, we would wrap them and place them under a small tree so we would have something to open in the morning. However, the day was usually filled with family and friends coming to visit, and we were able to enjoy the day without having to go to work and eating tamales all day long.

Our birthdays were just another day as well, but my mother always made sure that our birthdays were special, as she would always make us our favorite meal and baked a cake for the celebration. I can still taste the homemade cakes she would make from scratch. I missed those cakes while away at nursing school. One year, while at nursing school, she had bought me an outfit, mailed it to me, and it somehow was lost in the mail, so I never received a birthday present that year.

My early school years were basically uneventful. I dreaded the first day of school because none of the teachers could ever pronounce my name correctly. My first name, Pilar, was butchered so often, and my last name, Ybarra, was very hard for them to say. They would call me Pillar, Pielar, Peelar, everything but Pilar. So as they would struggle to call out my name, I would just raise my hand to let them know of my attendance. My appreciation of my first name did not come about until I grew up and realized it was different from so many other names, and I began to like it. But as a youngster, my wish was that my name be anything but Pilar. My friends would tease me and call me Pilaf, and I would just smile; my insecurity at an early age did not allow me to correct them.

I so wanted to bring my lunch to school in a lunch pail like the other kids, but my father insisted that we eat a hot lunch. As poor as they were, they somehow managed to find enough money so that we could all buy a hot lunch every day. The school allowed students to help serve in the cafeteria for a week at a time, and during that week, our lunch was free, so that helped. While we did not have the best and fanciest clothes, my mother made sure we were always wearing clean clothes. The flour she used to make tortillas came in a cotton sack, often with nice designs on the material. She would use the material to make clothes for us, and hand me downs were definitely put to good use.

My second-grade teacher once asked me if I knew what I wanted to be when I grew up and I told her that I wanted to be a nurse. I had no idea how this would happen considering how poor we were, but I remember seeing nurses in their starched white uniform and getting butterflies in my stomach. My mind would tell me that one day, I would be one of them.

While I had picked up the English language rather easily, my comprehension of some words or directions was not always what it needed to be. Memories of my third-grade teacher once kicking me with her knee as she was frustrated with me because I was not understanding a concept and kept asking questions still resonate with me even today. I was very hurt and embarrassed by that incident but never told my parents. I always tried to be very helpful and polite to my teachers and other students and was never in trouble at school.

My mother always helped all of us with our spelling; somehow even though she had little education, she knew how important it was for us to be able to spell correctly. So every Thursday evening, she would make us practice spelling the words that we would be tested on the next day. To this day, we are all good spellers and credit that to our mother.

During my fourth grade was when a dark period of my life started as I began to be sexually molested by a relative. Unfortunately, this continued through the years, and I was never able to tell my parents as they would not have believed me, so I just endured it. Not really understanding what was happening to me until later, I was too ashamed to say anything to anyone about it. My abuser would always tell me we had to keep it a secret between the two of us, and unfortunately, I believed him.

In the spring of my fifth-grade year, I was selected by a local club in town to attend summer camp with all expenses paid. Never having been to camp before, I did not know what to expect. That would be my very first time to be away from home, so I was scared and excited at the same time.

It was a wonderful week at camp, meeting new friends and learning how to do arts and crafts, row a boat, sit by a campfire, and roast marshmallows and other activities. I went to my first dance with a boy and thoroughly enjoyed the experience. After a week, it was time to go back to the reality of life, which meant working on my father's ranch, picking grapes and working hard. My later years of grammar school were filled with school activities. I became a cheerleader for our school, joined clubs like 4-H and the school orchestra, playing the violin. I was so proud when my parents were finally able to attend a musical presentation, and I played a solo on my violin. My parents could see that all my practicing had paid off even though I am sure that they had to endure times when my practicing sounded more like a bee flying around than music. As a seventh grader, my instructor selected me to be part of the Fresno County school orchestra along with students from other county schools. I met my dear friend Ana in this arena, and we have been best of friends ever since then.

Because we did not attend Catholic school, my mother made it a point to take us all to catechism classes each Saturday morning to learn about our Catholic faith. We would all climb in the car, and she would drop us off at the Catholic school where we had classes for ninety minutes. She would then return and pick us up and drive us home.

During the seventh grade is when Catholic students would begin to prepare to receive the sacrament of Confirmation. One Saturday while preparing for this sacrament, our parish priest, a big, tall Irish man with a booming voice stood right in front of me and in his deep voice asked, "Miss Ybarra, who is the mediator between us and God?" Now, not knowing what the word *mediator* meant and having been taught that there was good and evil, my response in a questioning manner was, "The devil?" At that point, in an even louder voice he told me to get out of his class and so I went outside and sat on a bench until my mother returned to pick us up. When she saw me sitting outside, she asked me why and I informed her about having been thrown out of class because of my response. I later realized that the correct response was Jesus Christ, but by then, it was after the fact. I did manage to make my Confirmation but never forgot that encounter and also never forgot the definition of the word *mediator*.

I had my first boyfriend and first kiss during eighth grade. While I had crushes on other boys beginning in the sixth grade, this was the first time I had actually kissed a boy. The romance was short-lived as summer vacation came along, and we were moving onto high school. While anxious about starting high school, I was ready to leave elementary school and move on with life. The one regret about elementary school was that my parents were never much involved with my school activities. My father had never attended school a day in his life, and my mother had only attended up to the eighth grade. She was also hard of hearing and was embarrassed about her disability, so the support for my school activities was not there. My mother was not even able to attend my eighth-grade graduation as she was home with my baby sister who had just been born. I tried to understand my parents' reasons for not being at my school activities and promised myself that when I had children of my own, attending their school activities would be of upmost importance knowing firsthand how important it was to have parental support.

Our summers consisted of working long hard hours out in the field on my father's ranches doing heavy work. There was no time nor money for vacations. All throughout grammar school, it was always embarrassing on the first day of school when kids were asked by the teacher to tell the class what they had done during the summer. Many of the students would tell of trips to the beach, Disneyland, the Grand Canyon, camping trips, or visits to New York, Florida, and other states. Our response was always the same, "We worked on our father's ranches." We were our father's workforce, so every school holiday and vacation, we were always working. If we were lucky, we might get to go visit our aunts and uncles on my mother's side of the family in San Jose for a week. While we despised working in the field, it gave us an opportunity to bond closer to our mother and brothers and sisters, and my mother always used the time wisely giving us *consejos* (wise advice) that we still live by today.

Graduating from the eighth grade at age thirteen and not wanting to have to work on my father's ranch, I applied for a job packing fruit at a packing house in a nearby town. My two aunts worked there, so I lied about my age, telling the boss that I was sixteen instead of thirteen and went to work with my aunts just to get away from working out in the field. However, being too young, I was not able to keep up with the pace of the workload, and after a couple of weeks of work, was laid off, so it was back to the field.

Being the oldest of six, I had to work just like a boy, lifting heavy items, and doing the work that was meant for men. Thus, I never knew the glamour of doing girl things like learning how-to put-on make-up or shopping for clothes, attending sleepovers, going to the movies, and just hanging out with friends. There was no time for such play.

As mentioned earlier, my parents raised us up in the Catholic faith, and every night we would all pray the rosary together in Spanish. Praying the rosary in Spanish was very stressful for me as I could not pronounce all the words of the Our Father correctly, and my father always made it a point to stop the rosary and make me repeat the words. Other times, he would yell at me for not being able to pronounce the words correctly. I tried my best but seemed to have a mental block and was always in trouble with my father for my inability to say the prayer to his satisfaction. My parents would bless each of us every night after the rosary, but when my father would get upset with me, he would refuse to bless me. I would wait to receive his blessing, but waited in vain and finally would just move on to receive my mother's blessing. His actions so traumatized me that even today, I still get stressed when attending a funeral of a Spanish speaking relative and the rosary is prayed in Spanish. Being the only one singled out and not being blessed even though I know that my brothers and sisters could not say all the words correctly, either was very difficult. Maybe that is what happens when you are the oldest of six children. This definitely left a deep impact on me and brings back many sad memories of my childhood. I really tried to learn all the words and pronounce them correctly, but I must have had a mental block because I just never could say the entire Our Father prayer in Spanish correctly. I would cry myself to sleep on many nights after being chastised and unblessed by my father. I could never quite understand why he could be so cruel, and after a while, I just quit asking for his blessing.

CHAPTER 3
High School Years

Starting high school was a totally new experience. While most of my grammar school friends attended the same high school, there were many more students from other schools in attendance. There were so many new people around the school and in my different classes. Moving from one class to the other was also a different experience from sitting in one classroom for the entire day. I soon made new friends to hang around with, as many of my old friends from grammar school were not in my high school classes. I found myself competing with different individuals and had to learn a new way of getting to and from classes on time. I was in awe of the upperclassmen as they seemed to get around campus easily and stress-free. Because we lived in the country, I would ride the school bus to and from school every day. If I wanted to stay after school for an activity, I could not as I did not have a ride home. I was only allowed to participate in activities that were during school hours. The distance from school also kept us from being able to attend football games as my parents would not take us and come and pick us up. Once in a great while, my dean of students would feel sorry for me and would come by and pick me up so I could go to the football game. I think that in my entire four years of high school, I only attended five football games. The same was true for school dances. My friends would all get to go, but I had to stay home. I loved music and I remember dancing in my room by myself pretending I was at the dance. I would hear stories from my friends about how much fun they had, and all I could do was smile.

Two of my aunts had gone off to college—one to nursing school in the Bay Area and the other to Fresno State. My one aunt in nursing school had met a married man, fell in love, and dropped out of school. My other aunt met a man, got pregnant and dropped out of Fresno State. Therefore, I took the brunt and suffered because of their behavior so my father controlled my activities with an iron fist. I tried to understand his concerns but felt I had been cheated from enjoying my years of high school. My first year of high school went by fast, and before I knew it, I was a sophomore.

I began my sophomore year being thankful that we were no longer the new kids on the block. While we were not upper classmen yet, at least we were no longer freshmen. Classes were getting harder, and I found myself having to spend more time with my studies, especially in Spanish. While I was bilingual, Spanish II consisted of conjugating all of the verbs which just did not make sense to me, so I really struggled with that subject. I continued to join school clubs and participated in as many events as possible during school hours. New teachers had different expectations, and some were hard to please, but I kept trying. My grades were holding steady despite my working on the ranch. There was envy on my part of my classmates who did not have to work as hard and who were able to truly enjoy their high school years.

Toward the latter part of my sophomore year, I was called into my counselor's office to discuss my plans for the future. He asked me, "What do you want to pursue when you graduate?"

My quick response was, "I want to be a nurse."

My counselor looked at me strangely, shook his head, and said,

"No, you are poor, you are Mexican, you are going to be a secretary."

Looking at him with a puzzled face, my response was "I don't want to be a secretary, I want to be a nurse."

His response to me was, "We know best," and with those words, my curriculum for the rest of my high school years was set. If those words would be said in today's times, they would probably be considered discriminatory, but this was the 1960s when very few people challenged authority.

Consequently, my junior year's curriculum consisted of all secretarial type courses, typing, shorthand, business—all classes which were easy for me. I found that I loved typing and was typing and taking shorthand at eighty to ninety words per minute. But while the classes were truly enjoyable, they had not changed my mind as to my goal of becoming a nurse. I saw education, and specifically a nursing career, as a way to get out of poverty, and here was my counselor trying to take my dream of becoming a nurse away from me. How dare he do that! Not knowing who to tell or who to discuss this with at the time, I just kept my feelings to myself, telling myself that someday, somehow, my goal of becoming a nurse would come to fruition. I joined the Future Nurses' Club, and the school nurse became my mentor, and she would encourage me to stay focused on becoming a nurse. She informed me that the local hospital was starting a first ever candy striper class, and I begged my parents to allow me to become one. A uniform was required, and I was not sure that my parents would be able to afford it, but with some luck they were able to buy the uniform. A feeling of pride and happiness came over me when I put on the uniform for the first time and went to volunteer at the hospital. I loved volunteering and working with the patients; this confirmed for me that I truly wanted to be a nurse.

After turning sixteen, my ability to apply to work in a packing house became a reality, and I was able to get a job at a local packing house during the summer; anything to get me out of the fields. I managed to hold on to my job this time and made adequate money which was set aside for school. However, as students, we were only allowed to pack tree fruit, so when the season was over in late July, we were laid off and had to find other employment. So back to the fields I went again. During the peak of the season, we worked long hours in the packing house, working overtime and even double-time. That was when we could make the most money, but it was very tiring. I would look at the women who came back year after year to work in the packing houses and wondered how they did it with no hope of making a change in their life. My future looked different than theirs, and for that, I was happy and grateful.

Winter vacations were always hard as we had to work out in the cold, under sometimes freezing conditions. My father would wake us up at five thirty in the morning, and we would be out in the field pruning the vines by 7:00 a.m. My father would get an old tire, and we would light a fire with wood inside the tire and pull it along the row as we moved from vine to vine to help keep us warm. My mother would make us burritos that we would have for lunch after warming them on the grill over the fire. They were simple burritos, but they tasted so good and warmed us up as we tried to keep warm next to the fire. Since I never learned how to prune the vines correctly, my father would send me to tie the vines. I was good at this and very fast, but every once in a while, one of the vine branches that had just been tied would come lose and snap back and hit me across the face. The sting of the hit was very painful as it was very cold, and my face felt frozen. My anger would get the best of me and so I would break the vine branch in half; luckily, my father never found out about the broken vine. When I was out by myself tying vines is when my mind would allow me to daydream the most and tell myself that someday I would no longer have to work this hard out in the cold. I could not wait for that day to come.

My father grew Thompson grapes for raisins, and sometimes, when it would threaten to rain and the grapes were still drying on the ground, we had to work very fast and hard to roll up the trays so they would not get wet. It gets dark earlier in the fall so to have light and keep on working, we would use the car lights so we could see what we were doing trying to roll up the trays. We would work until about 8:30 or 9:00 p.m. before we could go home, and once home, we would eat dinner and then we still had to study in order to keep up with our grades. Now my father did not like to see anything lower than a B on our report cards, but it was hard to work late into the night and then have to come home and do homework. Since my father worked the night shift at the time and got off at 3:30 a.m., I would leave him a note and ask him to wake me up when he got home in order to get up to study. During the winter, he would add more wood to the wood heater—our only source of heat—so it would be nice and warm for me. This action allowed me to maintain my *A*'s and *B*'s. It helped getting up early in the morning to study as the information was fresh in my mind, and it definitely helped me pass my tests.

Working for my father was never easy. He had finally been switched to the day shift at work, and now, he was home in the evenings. He pushed us very hard, never seemed to be satisfied with the amount of work done and would tell his relatives that we were lazy. If we did something wrong in his eyes, we were spanked with a cane from one of the vines. I was slapped often and told in Spanish that I was stupid and dumb. We never knew what type of mood he would be in when he came home from work. While we might be sitting in the kitchen talking with our mother after school, as soon as we saw him pull into the driveway, we would leave and go to our room and would stay there until we had to come out to help with dinner. If we were working on the ranch with him and wanted to tell him something that had happened at school, he would stop us and tell us this was not a time to talk but rather a time to work. I, along with my brothers and sisters, experienced emotional, physical, and verbal abuse from him. It took me many years of my adult life to forgive him and realize that he did not know any better as he had been abused by his father as a child. Thank goodness for our mother who, in her own way, showed us the love that we were desperately seeking.

As a senior in high school, I would sometimes spend the night at my aunt's home as my uncle worked nights every other month, and she did not like to stay alone at night. My girlfriend who lived down the road came over one evening, and we decided to trim my long hair as it would be easier to take care of when getting ready for school. When I went home and my father noticed that my hair was shorter, he became very angry. He decided that I needed to be punished for cutting my hair and found some rocks, laid them on the floor in front of our altar where the family prayed, and then made me kneel on the rocks with my arms outstretched for a long period of time. I could not drop my arms and the pain from the constant extension was excruciating. It was hard to understand the punishment as my only action had been to trim my hair. I remember asking him amidst my tears why he was being so mean but did not receive a response. My feeling was that this was cruel and unusual punishment and decided to run away from home. I packed a few things in a bag and took off on my bicycle. I did not get very far however, as my mother realized what had occurred and came after me to bring me back home.

Another time while working out on the ranch with him, my nose kept running and running. I ran out of Kleenex and so was sniffling and when he got tired of my constant sniffling, he came to me and squeezed my nose so hard that it made my nose start to bleed. I felt so hurt and wondered why he was so mean to me. Later, my allergy test showed that I was allergic to dust, and this is why my nose kept running; it was beyond my control. These experiences taught me that this amounted to child abuse and promised myself that someday when I had children of my own, they would never be treated in this manner.

Working in the fields also taught me that there was another way to make a living other than picking grapes, tying vines, and shoveling grass, and that was by getting a good education. I knew for sure that going to college was the answer, and this was the beginning of my transformation. Later, we realized that working so hard in the field was our father's way of making us hate field work so that we would go to college; reverse psychology, I guess.

My senior year, I was placed in a work-study program for two periods for the entire year. My counselor's goal was still to prepare me to become a secretary upon graduation. Against my wishes, I was sent to be a secretary for a local Catholic school. I would walk to the school, do secretarial work for the two periods there, and then return to the high school for the rest of the day to attend my other classes. Working for the nuns at the Catholic school reinforced my belief that I was absolutely positive that I did not want to be a secretary. I learned how to use the various pieces of secretarial equipment that were available at the time, like the mimeograph machine, the use of carbon copies, copy machines, etc. It seemed that no matter how much work was done for the nuns, they always had more work waiting for me to do. It was boring, and I resented being there, but did as directed all the while telling myself that someday I would be a nurse, not a secretary. I could not understand why my counselor was insisting on me becoming a secretary and wondered how many other students, particularly minority students were being forced to pursue careers that were not of interest to them.

I was not very assertive when in high school. While growing up, we were told not to speak until we were spoken to; it was considered disrespectful. We were taught to respect our elders as they usually knew better and what was best. Consequently, when we were given a directive, we usually did as we were told. To keep my mind off of what I was being pushed into, I joined a number of student organizations and became involved in school activities and committees. I even ran for school office in both my junior and senior years. Unfortunately, I was never successful in winning an office.

Graduation day finally arrived, and my parents were going to give me a party. They could not afford both a gift and a party, so I had saved enough money to buy myself a watch, which was what I wanted and bought it. My aunts and uncles jointly bought me my first record player. Loving to listen to music, I had always wanted one so was ecstatic when this gift arrived. This was the best gift I had ever received.

When it was time to preregister for college, I was somewhat at a loss as to what classes to register for my first year. Not having anyone in my family to ask advice of, I did my best. Knowing that science classes would be a must for nursing school, anatomy, physiology, psychology, and sociology were classes selected. I prayed that my actions had been correct. When my senior year was completed and scholarships were handed out, I was given a full-ride scholarship to a nine-month program at a business school; they were still pushing me to become a secretary. Disappointed, I kept my cool and promptly returned the scholarship to the school.

When my father found out about me returning the scholarship, he asked me, "Why did you return the scholarship the school gave you? You know that we do not have the money to send you to college."

My emphatic response was, "But, Dad, I don't want to be a secretary, I want to be a nurse!"

His obvious question to me was, "And just how do you plan to do that?"

My immediate response was, "I have no idea. I just know I want to be a nurse."

That summer we were run out of our home by my grandfather. He had given my father a piece of land on his ranch to build our house on, and we had lived there for many years, but after an argument with my father, he told us to get out. So our parents found a home across the dirt road from my aunt and uncle on three acres that they bought and we moved. It was a small three-bedroom wood house, but at least we had a home. We had never been able to afford a telephone before, but this house had a phone, so for the first time, we were able to communicate with our friends via phone. Our family had finally arrived to the twentieth century. It was nice living right across the road from our aunt, uncle, and cousins, and life was good.

The summer after graduation I went back to working in the packing house through tree fruit season to earn money for college. After the tree fruit packing season was over, I again returned to the field to work. I remember getting a job picking tomatoes and berries, both very hard work. I hated both of these jobs, but when you need money, you are not able to be picky. Survival came through me, telling myself that someday I would have a good job, a nice home, and a nice new car. My daydreaming would somehow make the hard work easier and less painful. That hope was what kept me going.

While there was no charge for tuition at the local community college, there were student fees to pay and books to buy. I worked long hours that summer and saved all of my earned money to pay for my school expenses. September arrived soon, and it was time to start college. While excited and thinking everything was set, there was one big problem. My family only had one car and my father used it to go to work, and since we lived in the country about five miles from the college, getting to college was going to be a challenge. Looking at options, and since my sister was still in high school and riding the school bus, I decided to just ride the bus with her. My plan was to get off at the high school and walk to the college just down the street. That worked for about two weeks until it was discovered that I was no longer a high school student and was informed that riding the bus was not allowed. So now what? How would I get to college now? Luckily for me, one of my friends who lived out by me had her own car, and she offered to pick me up and take me to school. This was a good solution, but the only problem was that I would have to fit her school schedule, so sometimes that meant going to school early or staying late until her classes were done and she could drop me off. Oh well, at least I had a ride.

My mind was still set on becoming a nurse but had no idea where I would go to nursing school. I was not even aware that two colleges in nearby towns each had a nursing program. I did not even know who to ask for advice. However, my uncle who lived in San Jose knew of a nursing program at a San Jose hospital and told me I should apply to that school. Not knowing much about the school, my decision was that I might as well apply and hope for the best. An application was submitted to the school, and after a month, I received an invitation to visit the nursing school. I had to take an entrance exam, and because math was my lowest score, a requirement for admittance was to take a remedial math class, which was done. If a student met the qualifications for admission, then a one-on-one interview would be scheduled in the future before a final decision for admission would be made. All I could do now was hope and pray.

Finals for the semester were coming up, and on the Friday before finals week, I brought all of my textbooks home with me to study. That night my father's Veterans of Foreign Wars organization was holding a Christmas dinner for members and their family. We all went and had a good time, and Santa Claus was even there passing out presents to all the kids. It was very foggy as we left to head back home that night, and as we were getting closer to our home, we could see what looked like a cloud of smoke. When we pulled into our driveway, we saw that our house was engulfed in flames. We quickly got out of our car, and my father and I tried to go into the house. All I wanted was to get all of my textbooks out of my room along with my record player. I had never had a record player before, and I treasured it. I tried to get back into my room, but the smoke was just too much, and I had to turn back and get out of the house. I stood there with my family and watched as our house burned to the ground. All we were left with was the clothes we were wearing on our backs; everything else was gone. We were left homeless with no place to go; a family of eight (six children and two parents) is not easy to place. We moved in with my aunt and uncle who had four children of their own, and all fourteen of us lived under one roof for two weeks until my parents were able to find new housing for us.

I was totally depressed. My books that I had brought home to study with and was planning to turn back in to the book store in order to buy new books for the next semester were all gone. I thought that my chances to go to nursing school had just vanished in the fire. I wanted to give up, but people in a small community are very good, and they all rallied around us, bringing us food, furniture, clothing, and utensils to help us get back on our feet. The churches gave us money and other organizations also gave us money. One local organization, the Lions Club came to my father and gave him a $200 check to help us. They wanted us to use half the money to buy clothes and the other half to buy kitchen utensils, and they asked my father to cash the check as soon as possible. We gladly and appreciatively accepted the donation. I remember my mother taking us to the local JCPenney store where we were able to buy two new outfits a piece. We had already been to the Salvation Army store and picked up some clothing to at least give us a couple of changes of clothes. Unfortunately, when the Lions Club found out that my father owned two ranches, they asked for their donation back; they felt we did not need it! We could not understand how the fact that my father had two ranches could replace the things that we had just lost and the clothing we needed right away. My father, being the proud man that he was repaid the money in full, and I have never forgotten this incident. Shame on the Lion's Club.

When we finally were settled in our new home, I told my mother that I assumed that I would not be able to travel to San Jose for my interview at the nursing school. She informed me that my assumption was wrong and gave me money to get to San Jose. I went up on a Greyhound bus and was picked up and taken to the interview by my uncle. I passed the interview with flying colors, and my dream of attending nursing school and becoming a registered nurse was coming true, and I was on cloud nine.

In early February of 1965, I found out that I had been accepted to the nursing school for the cohort that would begin in September 1965. I was so excited I could hardly contain myself but brought myself back to earth when I realized that I still had to finish my current semester. My parents were surprised and happy for me. As September came closer, I became more and more nervous and excited at the same time. I kept asking myself if I was in a dream, would I be able to make it through the program, what if I failed. What made matters worse was my mother telling me that if I failed I would not only be disappointing my family but my entire hometown—now, if that was not a guilt trip, I don't know what was.

CHAPTER 4
Going off to Nursing School

When the day finally arrived for me to leave, our family car had a lot of miles on it and could not have made it up Pacheco Pass to get to San Jose, so my mother and I took the Greyhound bus. I was scared to leave home, my brothers and sisters, and my friends. My fear of not wanting to let anyone down was almost paralyzing, but I was determined to reach my goal. Since the fire had burned all of our possessions, we only had one suitcase which could not accommodate all of my clothing. So I did the next best thing: I packed the rest of my clothes in a cardboard box wrapped with twine. Since I no longer had a record player, I had bought myself an AM/FM radio which I tucked under my arm. Imagine the looks on my new classmates' faces as I walked into the lobby of our dorm with a suitcase and cardboard box tied with twine. The looks on their faces were like, *Where did this country hick come from?* As I looked around the lobby and dorm, I did not see anybody who looked like me. Being the only Hispanic in my class, I felt quite alone but was determined not to throw away my chance of reaching my dream of becoming a registered nurse.

I was assigned to my dorm room and met my new roommate, Jeannie, who lived in San Jose along with other nursing student classmates. I met a girl named Jeanne from San Luis Obispo who was very friendly along with another girl from Gilroy. I remember meeting her in the bathroom and asking her what her name was and she responded, "Teddie."

Thinking this was her nickname, I asked her again, "So what is your real name?" and she again responded sounding a little irritated and said, "My name is Teddie."

Since my mother was in town, my aunts and uncles were getting together for dinner and invited me to join them, but I declined, deciding instead to hang out with my new friends. The next day, there was a reception for all the new students and their parents. My mother came with one of my aunts and uncles to the reception and introductions to my new roommate and her parents were made. Soon, the reception was over, and it was time for my mother to leave. I gave her a long hug and kiss before she left. I hated to see her leave and felt alone and afraid but realized that this was now my new home. I had to make the best of it. Tears ran down my face as she blessed me, and soon, she was out the door. I was now on my own.

The first day of class was quite an experience as we interacted with all the new classmates; they were from different parts of the state. We met our director, faculty, and house staff. We were told that not all of us would make it through the program as it was a difficult course of study, and we would have to work hard in order to be successful. They told us the truth, as we started with thirty-six students but ended our freshman year with only twenty. We were given our uniforms and textbooks and placed in our first course, Fundamentals.

In nursing school, we were assigned roommates, and mine was a girl named Jeannie. Her family actually lived in a classy area of San Jose, and her mother had been a nurse. Her mother would often come by while we were in class and leave homemade brownies on her bed. My roommate was friendly and nice but had poor study habits. The rules of the dorm were that we were supposed to keep our rooms neat and clean with our beds made; otherwise, we could receive demerits. Surprise checks were made by the housemothers and notes/demerits were left in our room. Because my roommate did not like to make her bed and her stuff was strewn all over her side of the room, we each would receive a demerit. After determining that she was not going to change and after getting tired of the demerits, I asked to have my own room. I was granted my request and never received another demerit.

My roommate's study habits were a problem for her. Every evening when we returned from class and dinner, she would say that she needed to make a list as to what she needed to do that evening before she could study. So she would begin to write her list, but she would get interrupted and would never finish her list. Consequently, she never had sufficient time to study. She did well in our clinical rotations but would fail her written tests. She was placed on probation, and she tried harder, but making her list was very important to her so she continued her usual pattern.

Our first instructor was nice but stern, and she began her work to develop us into nurses. We were to pair up with a partner as we began learning the basics of nursing fundamentals. I paired up with my roommate and looked forward to working with her. We began by learning how to take vital signs (temperature, blood pressure, pulse, and respirations). Since our family did not have a thermometer in our house, when it came time for me to take my roommate's temperature, I did not know which end of the thermometer went under the tongue. When I asked her, she looked at me and said, "You're kidding, right?"

To which I answered, "No, I have never used one of these before." If my mother wanted to know if we had a temperature, she would ask us to breathe on her, and she would feel our forehead to determine whether or not we were sick. While being embarrassed by this situation, I soon got over it and moved on passing the basics of taking vital signs on patients with flying colors.

I tried to help my roommate study and would even invite her to go down to the library with me to do our homework, but she never could seem to find the time. She just kept saying that she needed to make her list before she could study. Unfortunately for her, she would fail her tests and flunked out of school after her first year. She was allowed to come back and try again, but after failing a second time, she was asked to leave the school, and she could not return. Eventually, she was admitted to the nursing program at the local community college and did graduate and became a registered nurse. Her family was very kind and gracious to me and would invite me over to their house for dinner and to special events. I was always very grateful for their kindness.

Many of my classmates had boyfriends, and since they lived nearby, they would see them on the weekends. My boyfriend lived back home, so we rarely saw each other. He was my first love, and I met him my junior year of high school through my best friend, Ana, who happened to be dating his brother. He accompanied me to both my high school junior and senior proms, and I fell head over heels for him. In November of 1965, he was drafted into the Army and was sent to Fort Ord in Monterey County for his basic training, and we were able to get together once during this time. We spent the day together before he returned to his army post. Shortly after that, he was transferred to Fort Benning in Georgia for training as a radio operator. This was during the time of the Vietnam War, which was ramping up, and we were worried that he would be sent to Vietnam at the conclusion of his training. However, God was looking out for him, and he was sent to Germany for the rest of his tour of duty. He was allowed a ten-day leave before being sent to Germany, and we managed to see each other a couple of times before he had to leave. He asked me to wait for him, and of course, I said yes. We promised each other that we would write, and we did so on a regular basis and I looked forward to receiving his letters. I would write to him about my experiences in nursing school, and he would tell me about his army experiences. I missed him but tried to keep my mind on my studies and was excited about the many new things there was to learn.

Being away from home was difficult. My parents could only afford to send me ten dollars every two weeks when my father received his paycheck, as they had bills to pay and five kids to feed.

I had to make those ten dollars stretch to buy my food. It was not fun to always feel poor and not be able to buy the items needed. However, when I came home for the first time, I took my typewriter back with me and soon realized that since I had the ability to type fast and loved to type, my extra money could be made by typing papers for my classmates who did not like to type. So on Friday and Saturday nights while they were out on a date or having fun, I would stay in my room and type their term papers, charging them twenty-five cents a page. Those were the days of carbon paper and white out, so if a mistake was made, it took time to fix it; it was not as easy as it is today with a computer where you can just backspace and retype. Since my classmates did not like to type and were willing to pay me for typing their papers, my typing skills were helping me make extra money and survive financially. Thus, my typing skills learned in high school paid off after all.

CHAPTER 5

University Classes

As nursing students, we were in the hospital five days a week. Our clinical classes were held at the hospital, which was located on the same campus as our dorm rooms. So every morning we would get up, shower, put on our student uniforms, and walk across the campus to our clinical rotation. Our theory classes, however, were held in the afternoons at Santa Clara University, about two miles away. Since none of us had a car, we needed to figure out our transportation to and from the university. We settled on taking the bus to and from school but had to transfer to another bus in order to get to the university campus. This caused problems for us, as often, the buses would be late, we would miss our transfer, and thus we would be late for class. We then decided we needed to change our transportation strategy and found a taxi cab driver that would take up to seven of us at a time in his taxi. He would be waiting for us at our dorm to take us to class and at the university when we were finished with our classes. Since all of us could only afford twenty cents a day one way for transportation, we would watch the meter closely and as soon as it turned to $1.40 and before it reached $1.50, we would get out of the taxi and walk the rest of the way. Some days when it was raining hard, he would feel sorry for us and would just turn off the meter and take us all the way to our class building; he was very kind to us. Unfortunately, he was caught carrying too many passengers and was fired. We all felt very bad that he had lost his job on our account, but now we needed to figure out another mode of transportation.

Lucky for us, one of our classmates was given a big old Buick named Big Bertha, and she was able to give us rides to class. We would pile twelve of us into this car, three in the front, five in the back seat, and another four of us sitting on top of the five in the back seat; a little uncomfortable, but we made it work. One day, the car ran out of gas on our way to the university in the middle of a busy intersection. Fortunately, there was a gas station on the corner so we all had to get out of the car and push it to the gas station. I can just imagine the look on drivers' faces as they watched all twelve of us pile out of the car. It was like, *How many people can you put in a Buick?*

During our first year, many of our classmates became homesick and left school. In fact, only about two-thirds of the students who started with our class actually finished the program and graduated. Homesickness also affected me, but knowing that I could not disappoint myself or my family, I had to hold it together and keep studying—failure was not an option! I loved to receive letters from my mother and my boyfriend, and they helped to allay my homesickness. Since my aunts and uncles lived in San Jose, I would sometimes be invited to their house to visit on the weekends and that helped to alleviate my homesickness.

My first year, I was not able to go home until Thanksgiving vacation, buying a bus ticket and taking the Greyhound bus home. My parents picked me up at the bus station. On the way home, it was a very dark night, and as my father was driving down a very dark road, all of a sudden, there was a big cow in the middle of the road and my father was unable to stop in time. The car hit the cow causing it to fly up in the air, and it fell down next to our car. Thank goodness it did not land on top of us. The whole front end of the car was demolished, and we had to call for a ride home. I was so happy to see my family and eat a home-cooked meal. The days went by fast, and soon, I had to leave and go back; my next time home would be during the Christmas vacation but being home and seeing my brothers and sisters over the holiday gave me the boost to make it until the Christmas break.

We were given two weeks off for Christmas, and I again went home on the bus. During vacation, we worked out in the cold field tying vines again, but being able to be with my family made it worthwhile.

Our first year of the three-year program was not easy. We had to get used to the routine of nursing school and learn the basics of nursing care. I was away from home for a long time, and it was difficult. Many of my classmates were from the surrounding area so they had their friends and boyfriends to see on the weekends; I had my typewriter. It was especially lonely when most of them went home for the weekend, and the dorm was basically empty. When invited to one of my aunts' or uncles' homes for the weekend, I was really grateful for the invitation.

Thoughts of leaving crossed my mind on numerous occasions but knew that leaving was not the answer. Not having much extra money, going to the malls to shop was not an option, so rather than be tempted, I just stayed in the recreation room and watched television. I was happy for Sunday evenings as my classmates would return back to the dorm, and the dorm was lively again.

Our first year, we learned the basics of nursing care, like how to make a bed correctly with square corners. In order to pass this part of the class, our fundamentals instructor needed to be able to bounce a quarter off the bed; it took me a few tries before I was able to pass this part of the class. We also had to learn how to make a bed with a "patient" in the bed which was not an easy task. We learned how to take vital signs on our patients and how to give a patient a bed bath correctly. We had classes Monday through Friday, but Wednesdays we were given half a day off. As the months passed, my confidence in my abilities grew and my skills improved.

I enjoyed my studies and had a good basic understanding of anatomy and physiology as my full semester of each at Reedley Junior College had given me a good foundation. I felt sorry for my classmates as the university was on the quarter system, and they received only one quarter of both anatomy and physiology *together*. Thus sometimes, they were lost when trying to understand the concepts, and I was glad to help them. One classmate in particular had a very difficult time understanding some of the concepts, and I remember spending many hours trying to help her grasp the function of the body. Somehow she would manage to pass her classes, but it was always very stressful for her. We also had to take religion courses as this was a Catholic university. I struggled with my Gospels class, and my father was not happy when he saw the C grade for this class on my report card. I was just happy to have received a passing grade. We were taught by Jesuit priests, and when they began talking about the 4 gospels, I asked, "What four gospels? I thought there was only one?" They blew my mind with their teachings and made me think about my religion in a different way than the little I had learned in catechism when I was young.

I became involved with our school organizations and enjoyed meeting and working with the upper classmates at the school. We had several social events and raised money for our class by having bake sales and dinners. I remember having an enchilada fundraiser dinner for our class. We made money and had fun with this event. Our dorm had a TV and game room that was not often used except in the evenings when we had some free time. Many of us would gather in this room and share stories, laugh, and enjoy each other's company. We learned from each other, and I had my ears pierced for the first time by one of my classmates. She just took a piece of ice, froze my ear lobe, stuck a needle through it, and I now had pierced ears! There was only one phone in the hallway for all the girls to use, so it was busy in the evenings with all the personal phone calls. We had a curfew of 10:00 p.m. during the week and later on the weekends. The housemother on duty made sure that we came in on time and would report us if we did not. Many a time we would open the backdoor for one of our classmates who was late coming back to the dorm. We had joint shower and bathrooms in the middle of the long hallway. Our uniforms were washed by the hospital laundry, but we were responsible for doing our own personal laundry in the machines that were available for our use.

We were allowed to keep snacks in our room, but if we did not keep our door closed, the snacks sometimes would become a treat for Rocky, the big white Siberian Husky dog that belonged to the nuns and would sometimes get loose from his yard and come into the dorm and go searching for food. We had a dislike for this dog who had no trouble coming into our dorm room and finding our snacks. The nuns loved their dog, and the rest of us just had to put up with him and pretend we liked him too. One day, Rocky got loose and took off running across the street. The nuns were going crazy trying to find him and bring him back; we were hoping that he would be gone for good, but alas, he did come back home.

Toward the end of our freshman year, my classmates and I were invited to a fraternity party at San Jose State. There I met a guy from Wisconsin who was in the Air Force and stationed at the Air Force Almaden base on top of the hills of the Santa Clara Valley. We were both lonely and quickly hit it off and began dating. I did not tell him about my boyfriend in Germany and did not tell my boyfriend about the new guy. I figured this relationship would be short-lived and would be over by the time my boyfriend would return back to the USA.

Our first year of nursing school ended almost as fast as it began. We had learned the basics and were now able to work in a hospital as a nursing assistant. I was elated to have successfully completed my first year of study and knew that, for me, going to nursing school was the right decision. Returning home that summer, working in the packing house or the fields was no longer necessary. Instead, I was hired by my local hospital to work as a nursing assistant on the night shift. Up until this point, I had not been a coffee drinker but soon learned how to drink black coffee in order to stay awake during the night, especially on slow nights.

CHAPTER 6
Surviving My Second Year in Nursing School

September came around soon, and I was happy to return to nursing school. The first night we were back, my Air Force friend called and asked if he could come and see me. He brought over a couple of friends who were introduced to a couple of my nursing school friends. It felt good to see him, and I was happy to be back.

My father, realizing that transportation to and from the university was a problem, let me take an old car with me that he had purchased. It was an old Ford Falcon that needed a new engine and smoked like a chimney, but it ran well enough to use to go back and forth to school. I was able to drive some of my classmates to the university and would charge them fifty cents a week for gas. The car even managed to make it to San Francisco on a weekend for some fun, but on the way back, the accelerator got stuck, and I had to drive holding down the brake most of the way back on the freeway. However, my classmates who were with me in the car were not made aware the situation. I was so happy when we got back to our dorm safe and sound.

Because our program was only a three-year diploma program, we did not have a sophomore year but went from being a freshman to a junior. We had a couple of new students who joined our class that year as they had failed their junior year and were now joining our class. They were welcomed to our class and soon became one of us. However, one of them was very verbal about her feelings about minorities and would often make comments to me that were hurtful, and being the only minority in my class, I felt alone. Finally, after hearing enough of her comments, my anger got the best of me, and I was able to tell her how she was making me feel and told her she better stop before she made me really mad and I might do something that I would regret. Her response was that she did not think of me as being Mexican; I told her that she better start. She did not bother me after that. While she probably still made comments when I was not around, at least my ears did not have to hear her hurtful words anymore. We have since become good friends, and she even apologized to me for the hurtful things she had said to me in the past.

I was missing my boyfriend and the separation fed into my loneliness. I continued to date the guy from the Air Force, and we both began to have feelings for one another. I learned that his father was a Methodist minister and he had several brothers and sisters back home. He accompanied me to several of our school events as well as our Christmas ball and prom. We would always have a great time and enjoyed each other's company. He and his Air Force buddies had an apartment in town that they shared, and my friends and I would often go there on weekends and make dinner for them and just hang out with each other.

Our classes became more challenging this year. We all had to take microbiology, and unfortunately for us, we were placed in the class with biology majors. Needless to say, none of us did well in this class and were called to a meeting with the nun director of the school who informed us that there did not have to be a senior class the next year. In other words, get it together and start passing this course, or we would all be dropped from the program. We asked to be placed in a different class, and our request was honored. After receiving tutoring, we all managed to pass microbiology.

Our clinical classes included obstetrics and gynecology, which were very enjoyable, and psychiatric nursing—which I did not enjoy. Our obstetric instructor allowed us to pick a patient and "follow" the same patient during our fifteen-week rotation in this subject matter. I picked a patient who was due to deliver around Thanksgiving, and in fact, went into labor the night before Thanksgiving Day. Thus I had to stay with her until she delivered her baby the next morning and was not able to go home for the holiday until she had delivered. Falling in love with obstetric nursing, my plan was to work in this area upon graduation.

Psychiatric nursing was a different matter. We were sent to Agnew's State Hospital for our clinical experience. On our first day there, we had to select a patient that we wanted to follow from observation only; we could not look at the patient's chart until after we had made our selection. Imagine my surprise when discovering that the patient I had chosen was a registered nurse. My immediate thought was, *Oh my god, that is going to happen to me!*

We received both clinical and theory grades for this course. I did just fine in my clinical phase. My original patient selected was transferred to a different facility so this required me to select another patient. I chose an elderly man who would not let anyone stand or sit close to him. His underlying disease was Parkinson's, so his hand would always shake. If I tried to sit next to him, he would get up and move to another location. While my early efforts were initially rejected, little by little, I was able to first stand and then sit next to him. After some time, he finally allowed me to sit next to him for longer periods of time and hold his shaking hand. I was able to make small progress with him each day. Toward the end of my clinical rotation, he finally allowed me to sit next to him and talk to him while holding his shaking hand. I felt sad when our rotation at the psych facility ended, and we had to leave since I would never see him again.

One of the procedures that was not enjoyable in my psych clinical rotation was having to assist the doctors administer electric shock therapy to some of the patients. It appeared to be a cruel type of treatment, and I was not convinced that it actually helped patients, but being only a student I had no say in the matter.

The hospital was cold and the doors slammed shut. Many years later when seeing the movie, *One Flew Over the Cuckoo's Nest*, it gave me chills as it brought me right back to my student days when you would hear the keys to the locked doors dangling and the heavy doors close behind you. Though sad to leave the elderly man with Parkinson's, I was happy to finish this rotation, knowing that psychiatric nursing would not be my job of choice.

While doing very well in my clinical work, my written tests were very challenging for me as the questions were difficult to understand. My instructor told me that while doing excellent work in the clinical arena, my comprehension of the theory portion was a different matter. Since passing this class depended on both clinical as well as theory grades, my test grades would have to improve. With much prayer and more study, I managed to pass my psychiatric rotation but knew that if I failed the state board exam, it would be due to the psychiatric portion. In those days, there were five sections to the nursing state board exam: medical, surgical, obstetrics, pediatrics, and psychiatric, and they were each individually graded. In order to pass the exam, you needed to pass all five sections before you could be issued a license as a registered nurse. Luckily, I did manage to pass my state board with flying colors but received my lowest score in the psychiatric portion.

In the spring of my junior year, I began to have abdominal pains of unknown origin. I ended up in the emergency room on three separate occasions, and finally, after my third visit, I was referred to an obstetrics/gynecology doctor. He admitted me to the hospital, and after running some tests, told me that he would have to do an exploratory laparoscopy in order to find out what was causing my pain. In the '60s, there were no ultrasound or CAT scans available to identify the problem like there are today. Surgery was the only option. My mother came up to be with me, and when the nun director of the nursing program found out that I would have to have surgery, she informed me that if I had to be out of school longer than two weeks, that I would have to repeat my entire junior year. Now, I knew that my parents were struggling to pay for my tuition, so to ask them to pay for my junior year again was not acceptable to me. So when the nurse came into my room to have my mother sign my surgical consent, I told her to get out of my room that I was not going to have the surgery. Of course, she immediately called my doctor who called me and told me that I needed the surgery to find out what was causing my pain. I informed him of what I had been told by the director, and he promised me that he would use special sutures to get me back to school as soon as possible. So reluctantly, I decided to go ahead with the surgery.

My doctor discovered that my pain was being caused by a dermoid cyst that had wrapped itself around my right ovary and fallopian tube so both had to be removed. The nun director, who was a registered nurse, actually scrubbed in for the surgery. I think she believed that I had an ectopic pregnancy and wanted to see with her own eyes. I was a patient in the hospital for one week. The next week, I pressed my doctor for permission to return to class, and the following week, I was back in the hospital taking care of patients after having had major abdominal surgery. I lived on the second floor of the dorm and it only had stairs, no elevator, so every day I was having to walk up and down stairs as I held on to my abdomen to help calm my pain. I was determined that I would not be kicked out of school, and I received my highest grades that quarter. Even my doctor was surprised with my rapid recovery. I am sure that I probably hurt my body by returning to the clinical area as soon as I did, but at that point in my life, nothing was more important than graduating on time and with my classmates.

My new boyfriend was very concerned about me and kept calling me to see if I was awake on the day of my surgery. When he came down from the hill that evening to visit me in the hospital, my mother was at my bedside and so I had to introduce him to her. Her first question to me after he had left was what had happened to my other boyfriend who she knew and liked. She was concerned that I was dating two different men.

My best friend in nursing school knew about my boyfriend in Germany and told her boyfriend who was also in the Air Force and a friend of the new guy I was dating. My new boyfriend must have told him that he was falling in love with me and so his friend proceeded to tell him that I had a boyfriend in the Army who was stationed in Germany. The next day, when he came to visit me, he immediately said to me, "Tell me about the guy in Germany," and I had to tell him the truth. He became upset and did not call me for some time after that. I was told that he had begun to date another girl, and I figured that our relationship was over, so I was really surprised when he called me about two months later. He called me up and told me he had told the other girl that it was over between them. When I asked him why, he told me he wanted to continue to see only me so we reestablished our relationship. He asked me to go to Wisconsin with him, but I knew that could never happen. While I cared for him, I was not convinced that I loved him.

I returned home that summer and was rehired to work as a nursing assistant at my local hospital, this time on the p.m. shift. I worked as much as I could, saving all my money for my last year of nursing school. My new boyfriend continued to keep in touch by calling me at home and writing. I kept busy with work, and my father, who was very demanding, kept trying to run my life and make decisions for me even though I was twenty years old. At one point, I angered my father that summer, so when it came time to return to nursing school he told me that he would not be paying for my tuition. I was disappointed, sad, and scarred and wondered how I would manage to pay for the last year of nursing school. I was so close to reaching my dream that I could not let anything stop me now, but I knew that I had not made enough money that summer to cover my tuition. Thank goodness for my sister, Esther, who was three years younger than me. She had been accepted to the University of the Pacific and her tuition was being paid via scholarships and grants. She had worked three different jobs that summer, and she gave me all of the money she had saved so that I could finish up my nursing program. I was forever grateful to her for helping me, and I tried to help her once I got a job working as a registered nurse. To this day, I have not forgotten her generosity. My father often wondered how I had managed to pay for my schooling for the last year, and we never told him. I think he felt guilty for not helping me my last year, but as my mother always told me, where there is a will there is a way. So true.

In September, I returned for my final year. The first night I got back, my new boyfriend came to see me at the dorm. It was good to see him, and we began dating again. My boyfriend in Germany was due to be discharged in October, and I informed my new boyfriend of his upcoming discharge. I basically broke up with him, and shortly after that, he asked to be transferred back to Wisconsin to complete his tour of duty and he went back home. He asked me to move back there with him a third time, but I just could not see myself moving to Wisconsin, so we ended the relationship. My boyfriend did return from the Army as scheduled and I waited for him to call me, but he never did. Finally, I called him, and when he answered I asked him why he had not called me. He could not really answer the question other than to say he needed some time to get used to being home before calling me. I was disappointed with his answer but tried to understand his feelings. We made plans for me to come home the following weekend, and we went on our first date since his homecoming. Our relationship seemed strained, and I attributed this to our having been away from each other for almost two years. I felt that once we began dating again that things between us would get back to normal, but this did not happen.

CHAPTER 7

Final Year of Nursing School

Our senior year definitely helped prepare us for our future career. We took on harder assignments and were responsible for a larger number of patients. We had to develop care plans for our patients and demonstrate that we were able to care for their needs. This year included our pediatric experience. Now, I had dreaded pediatrics since I entered nursing school, and I was scared to death on my first day of clinical. My first assignment was a six-year-old little girl who had just been diagnosed with diabetes, Type 1. I had to teach her how to give herself her own insulin—not an easy thing to do when you are only six years old. After giving it much thought, I decided to make it into a game. I made her a nurse's cap out of paper and used an orange to teach her how to give the injections. She learned quickly, and by the time she left the hospital, she was injecting herself with only a little help required. I was very happy when our pediatric rotation was completed.

Medical/Surgical Nursing II was our last subject, and we learned how to care for more complex patients. One of my most challenging patients was an eighteen-year-old young man who had been burned. He was a farm worker from Los Baños who was working with some "friends" and was riding in the back of a station wagon on his way to another job. The station wagon had been carrying gasoline in five-gallon containers and some of the gas had spilled on the carpet.

His "friends" decided it would be funny to light a match and throw it on the carpet wet with gasoline. The spilled gas ignited and burned the young man over 30 percent of his body, and he was admitted to the medical/surgical floor as the hospital did not have a burn unit. The young man and his buddies had a history of drug abuse. He had been in the hospital for two weeks, and I was assigned to his care. He needed protein but was refusing to eat the high-protein diet that was provided for him. After talking to him about what he liked, he told me that the only thing he really liked was milkshakes, so I talked with the dietician and asked her to add eggs to his daily milkshakes in order to provide him with more protein. We made sure that he had all the milkshakes he wanted and his protein levels began to rise and his healing began to improve. He gained confidence in me and shared many stories about his life. One day he told me that he had decided to stop taking drugs as he realized the harm that they were doing to his body. This was great news, and so I quickly went out to find my instructor and informed her. Her wisdom and experience came through as she asked me if he had any recent visitors. I told her that a couple of his friends had just been visiting him, at which point she informed me that he probably just had a "fix" and that is why he was talking the way he was about quitting. Her experience and wisdom taught me a valuable lesson that day about how to use critical thinking in nursing. After questioning him, he admitted to me that he had just had a fix which had been brought in to him by his visitors. My instructor was very wise. She was also wise when she told us to never marry a doctor.

Each Friday morning, we had to meet with our senior instructor, and she would drill us about our patients to measure our understanding of the nursing care we were delivering. Several of my classmates were so nervous about meeting with her and being questioned that they literally got sick. I always managed to answer her questions correctly, so she did not really bother me. However, one time she asked me a question I could not answer, and at that point, she said, "Aha! I finally got you," and smiled. Needless to say, I never forgot the question or the lesson she taught me that day about learning absolutely everything about my patients.

Because our senior year was very busy, visits home to see my boyfriend were few and far between. The last time we went on a date to a drive-in movie, I sensed that something was wrong but did not want to address it. In April, my suspicions came true as he wrote me a Dear John letter telling me that he had met someone else, and he was breaking up with me. The news was devastating and led me to cry my eyes out. Here I had broken up with the guy from Wisconsin because he was coming home from the service, and now he informed me that he no longer was interested in continuing our relationship. I locked myself in my room for two days, and my classmates were worried about me, trying everything to coax me to come out. Finally, after tearing up all the pictures of the both of us, I came to my senses. Telling myself that I could and would not let some guy keep me from completing my senior year and finishing my nursing program, my life continued without him. I dated other guys and invited them to events in order to forget my old boyfriend.

Our senior year was finally over and graduation time was upon us. The morning of our graduation, my classmates and I went to the hospital cafeteria to eat breakfast as we usually did. On the way back to our dorm room, we were walking past the chapel, and I asked them to go back to the dorm without me as I wanted to stop by the chapel and give thanks. I vividly remember kneeling and giving thanks to God for allowing me to reach my dream of becoming a registered nurse and asking Him to help me pass my state board exam. My prayer of thanks included telling Him that I did not know where He would take me, but I would gladly go where He would lead me. Having given thanks, I left the chapel happy and went to my room to get ready for graduation.

CHAPTER 8

Finally, Graduation

Our graduation took place at Mission Santa Clara with its beautiful paintings, window art, and gardens. Our families were all there as eighteen of us received our diplomas. Each year, one graduate was awarded the top honor award at graduation. It came with a $50 gift. This year, I was lucky enough to receive this award based not only on my grades but also because of my determination to not let anything stop me from graduating on time. My parents and family were very proud of me for being the first one in our family to have attended college and graduate. I was so happy and proud to receive this recognition and used the money to help finance my trip for my volunteer work in Mexico that summer after taking the state board. My desire to go and volunteer in Mexico began the summer between my junior and senior years, but it required my parent's permission as I was not twenty-one years of age. My parents had refused to sign the permission slip, and thus, there was no trip to Mexico that summer. But now, having turned twenty-one and no longer needing their signature, I made plans to travel to Mexico that summer and volunteer with a group from the Bay Area known as Amigos Anonymous, a group similar to the Peace Corps.

After graduation, my parents gave me a big party inviting all of my relatives and my classmates to this event. My parents were so proud of me and were happy that their first child had graduated from college. I stayed at the dorms for one-week post-graduation to study for my state boards, and after a few days, decided the time to study had ended. If I did not know it by now, it was too late. My classmates and I traveled to San Francisco to take our state board exam. It was a two-day event, and we took a total of five different tests that were timed. The testing was done under strict supervision. If we needed to use the restroom, we had to raise our hand and ask for permission as only one person could go at a time. We were all exhausted after taking our state exam but were glad it was over. Now it was a waiting game until we were notified of the results, which would take about six weeks.

My original goal after graduation was to join the armed forces, either the Navy or Air Force and be a nurse. Recruiters informed me that a tremendous amount of experience could be gained and that nurses in the armed forces had a great opportunity to travel the world. However, both my parents were very much against this decision and said that no daughter of theirs would ever join the service. In their opinion, "good girls" just did not do that. Thinking that they probably knew best and not wanting to cause an argument, I dropped the idea and never pursued this again. When speaking with nurse colleagues who had joined the service and hearing their stories, I regretted my decision not to enlist. To this day, this is one of my only regrets about my career as a nurse.

My father was upset with me for not starting to work immediately. But needing a break from my studies, I traveled to San Diego to join two of my classmates who were also going to Mexico to volunteer. So it was off to Mexico traveling on a bus for almost three days to get to Morelia, Michoacán, to join a group of college kids from across the nation. Still grieving the loss of my boyfriend and not wanting to return back home for fear of running into him, the decision to leave for Mexico for the summer was an easy one to make.

Upon arriving at my destination, I was met by a coordinator who introduced me to the family I would be living with that summer. There were two small boys who volunteered to help me with my luggage for a tip. However, not yet knowing the exchange value of American money, the tip they actually received was just a small token. When this was pointed out to me later, it was embarrassing since the tip had turned out to be about fifty cents instead of five dollars. *C'est la vie.* The family who welcomed me had one son who was a priest and five daughters. I was given my own room and enjoyed living in a house with a courtyard in the middle of the home. Knowing and understanding the language, it was easy to converse with them, but sometimes my slang caused some problems for me. As an example, at my first dinner with the family, they asked me if I wanted more food and my response was, "*No, estoy llena,*" which in the United States means, "No, I am full," but in Mexico, it meant that I was pregnant. They all looked at me with questioning faces and realizing what had been said, I tried to explain and assure them that the person they had just welcomed was not pregnant.

The father of the family was never around, and when the daughters were questioned as to his whereabouts, the question was never answered. However, every Sunday, the family would send me to spend the day with another family, and they would go off the entire day and returned at night. I later learned that the father was in prison as he had owned a grocery store and someone had sold him some bad alcohol which he had sold to customers not knowing that the alcohol was bad, and a couple of people had died. So every Sunday, the family would go to visit him at the local prison, and they were too embarrassed to tell me.

On a long weekend, four of us girls took the train to Mexico City, and there we met up with their son, the priest, who finally told me about his father. My heart went out to them, and unfortunately, he was a stranger to me; we never met.

Working with the public health nurses, visiting people in the poor villages, and teaching health classes to mothers on health care filled up the day. It was a beautiful country, and the people were all very lovely and caring. Thoughts of staying in Mexico crossed my mind, and had I not already made a commitment to share an apartment with my old roommate and begin the new job waiting for me in San Jose in September, I probably would have stayed in

Mexico. My mother had received my state board test results at home, and she mailed them to me in Mexico. Pure elation and happiness filled my body when I opened the envelope reading the first line which told me I had passed the state board. However, as self-predicted, psychiatric nursing was the lowest score of my test results. But bottom line, I had passed and was a very happy camper. My dream had been realized. I contacted my Amigo friends and several of us went to a bar in the middle of the day to have a drink and celebrate my success. While not a common sight, we were four American girls sitting in a bar in the middle of the afternoon in Mexico, celebrating my achievement.

About three weeks before returning home, I contracted pneumonia and had to take antibiotics. Up to this point, I had been healthy, had not eaten from the street vendors in order to avoid getting sick. But working long hours in the rain, walking through mud puddles, and working with the poor people in the villages had worn down my resistance. I was able to see a doctor who examined me and prescribed Penicillin G, a thick white antibiotic that was given by injection. Since the doctors in Mexico do not have nurses working in their office to give the injections, patients had to pay people in the street who had learned how to give injections to perform the function. Since nurses are taught how to give injections, I decided to give myself my own injections in my thighs. In those days, Mexico did not yet have disposable needles and syringes, and thus after buying a glass syringe and needle, it was necessary to boil the needle after each injection to sterilize it. Each time the needle was sterilized, it became duller and duller, which made the injection even more painful each time. The cough continued after returning home, and consequently, oral antibiotics were continued.

When I returned home, my uncle was picking his grapes, and my father woke me up early that Saturday morning and said to me, "Let's go help your uncle pick his grapes."

Reluctantly, I got dressed and went to do as he asked. All the dust and dirt in the field exacerbated my cough, and I coughed even more than before. When we came home at noon to eat lunch, I made a decision that changed my life. Telling myself that I was now a nurse and no longer had to work out in the fields my decision was that I would not go back and pick grapes again. Informing my father of my decision was not easy, and while he was not happy, he never pushed me to go out to the field to work again. I was thankful for that and never again went out to the field to pick grapes to earn money. My field work was finally over!

CHAPTER 9

Starting a Career

In early September, I returned to San Jose and moved into an apartment with my roommate to begin my job as a new nurse at San Jose Hospital. Waiting until all of my classmates had decided where they were going to work before deciding where to work was my way of trying to isolate myself from them. Starting my new career was scary, and I did not want any of them to know if I made a mistake. I figured that if none of them were working at the same hospital, then they would not know about the error if I made one. However, while none of my classmates were working at San Jose Hospital, my fundamentals instructor from nursing school had students at this hospital, and I saw her often; so much for well-laid plans. My application to San Jose Hospital asked for a position in the obstetrics unit, but because there were no openings, I was offered a position on a medical unit working the evening shift. I accepted the position and figured that an opportunity to transfer to the obstetrics unit would come up in the future. Having my job in place, as well as my apartment, I decided to buy my first new car—my dream car—a blue 1969 Pontiac Firebird. The cost was $3500, and when my parents learned of my decision, they thought that I would not be able to afford it. My father had to cosign in order for me to get my car loan, and after much begging, he finally did cosign for the loan which allowed me to purchase my new car. My payments were only $86 per month, and since my salary would be $500 a month, it was within my budget. Receiving my first paycheck as a registered nurse was very exciting, but then I realized how quickly my money was spent when having to pay for my rent, car payment, utilities, food, etc. But I was happy and loved the work, my car, and making good money on a regular basis.

My role was as a novice nurse (a beginner) and often wished that I had at least six months to a year's experience under my belt; that would have made me feel so much better. I was warned about the doctors who used to like to get fresh with the new nurses and so was on my guard and would often go out of my way to avoid passing by them. After being oriented on the day shift, I was transferred to the p.m. shift and began to work under the supervision of the assistant head nurse. Unfortunately for me, she was pregnant, and after two months of working with her, she went on maternity leave. Her replacement was a Filipino nurse who had never worked in an American hospital before—talk about the blind leading the blind. Having a little more experience than her, I had to take the lead, and it was learning by the school of hard knocks. There was so much to learn, but I felt that our nursing school had prepared us well to perform the duties of a nurse.

One of the evening nurses who worked part-time and had been a nurse for many years was very helpful; however, she had her limits. One of our patients had an order to have a glass of wine in the evening before bedtime, something she was used to having in her home. This nurse absolutely refused to give her the glass of wine and would state that she did not go to nursing school to be a bar maid. So I would give the patient her glass of wine, and she was most happy. Another memory of my first year was having my first code blue. I had walked into the room and found my patient to be unresponsive. Realizing that a code blue had to be called, I managed to do that, and that was all. Other nurses and staff rushed into the room and began to do CPR while I stood there frozen. I could not move but was aware of what was going on around me. Unfortunately, despite the assistance given to the patient, she did not survive. I learned from this experience, and in the future, had no trouble functioning during a code blue.

One evening, around 10:00 p.m., we received a visit from the house supervisor who told us that the hospital had received a threat of a bomb that was hidden somewhere in the hospital and it would go off that evening. She asked us to search our patient's rooms looking for anything out of the ordinary. Since our patients had already been put to bed and were sleeping, I took my small flashlight and searched the floor around the beds and bedside stands trying not to awaken my patients. One of my patients had a two-pound box of See's candies on her bedside stand, and as I was looking for the bomb alongside her bed and bedside stand, she woke up, sat up in her bed, and stated, "If you wanted a piece of candy, all you had to do was ask!" I just smiled and walked out of her room; I could not tell her what was taking place as this would have upset and frightened her.

The nursing union was just starting to organize nurses when I started to work at this hospital, and I did not like their tactics. They were putting a lot of pressure on the nurses to join the union. My nursing cap was taken from me, a black armband was placed on my arm, I was instructed not to frequent the hospital cafeteria and was pressured to join the union. I was not happy with this situation and thought about leaving but enjoyed my job and the people working on the unit; however, the union tactics made it impossible for me to stay.

In early December, my sister Esther called me and told me that my old boyfriend had contacted her and wanted my phone number. She called me to ask whether she could give him my number. I was shocked to hear this and gave her permission to give him my telephone number. He called me and informed me that he had broken up with the girl he had been dating and realized how much he missed me and wanted us to get back together. While happy to hear from him, I was not sure about getting back together with him. Since the Christmas holiday was coming up and I was planning to go home for Christmas, we agreed to get together and talk further. I told him how much he had hurt me, he apologized and told me how bad he felt, but he wanted us to try again. We met on Christmas Day and had a good time, and he agreed to come to San Jose to spend New Year's Eve with me. Being scheduled to work that evening, I called in sick, and we went to the beach for the evening. While feeling guilty for calling in sick, I felt that spending the evening with him was more important. Coming home again the third week in January, we went out on a date and he asked me to marry him and I, of course, said yes.

Now my father never liked my boyfriend and now my fiancé. My mother liked him very much. My father wanted me to marry a doctor or someone who worked in a hospital rather than my fiancé who was a barber. He never really had much to say to him when he would come to pick me up to go out on a date and was not happy that we were getting married. He even told him to leave one time when he had come over to see me, and I told him that if he made him leave, that I would be leaving with him. He allowed him to stay.

CHAPTER 10

Returning Home

After working at San Jose Hospital for six months and getting engaged to my boyfriend back home, I decided to move back to my hometown and begin to plan for our upcoming wedding. Our plan was for me to get an apartment in Fresno close to the hospital, but my mother was against that, telling me that all good girls lived at home until they got married and that an apartment was out of the question. So reluctantly, I moved back home for six months, thinking that this was a mistake but did not want to disappoint my mother. Later, my thinking proved to be right.

Before moving back, I had applied for a job at the community hospital, interviewed with the manager on duty on the weekend, and was hired by her to work on the evening shift on a medical floor. After finally moving back home in March, I met with the Human Resources manager who looked at me and immediately told me, "I don't know if we can hire you; you are overweight."

I thought to myself, *Well, I can always go back to my previous hospital if needed*, but she informed me that she would take me to meet the manager of the medical floor and let her decide whether she would hire me. The manager hired me on the spot. For who else would ask to work the evening shift on a medical floor? After officially being hired by the floor manager, the HR manager told me, "Well, you have six months to lose weight; if you don't lose weight, then you are out of here."

I told myself, *Whatever*. Today, this would be considered discrimination, but again this was the 1960s and comments like this were allowed and there was nothing that could be done; times have certainly changed for the better.

My employment with Fresno Community Hospital began in March of 1969. I started on the day shift and was oriented by a very professional and kind nurse. She made sure that I had the opportunity to learn the processes of the medical floor before being scheduled to orient on the evening shift. Unlike the very nice nurse on the day shift, the nurses on evening shift were not so welcoming. My first day of work on the evening shift was a real eye-opener as to what my experience would be like. When entering the report room, the German nurse with whom I was scheduled to orient with told me that since the other nurse was not there yet, I needed to take report on the other team. Even though I explained to her that my role there that evening was to orient to the evening shift, she insisted that I had to take report on the other team. Finally, the other nurse came into the report room, and so I went back to the nurse that I was scheduled to orient with only to be told that she did not like to orient new nurses and she sent me back to the other nurse. Asking the other nurse if I could orient with her, she quickly responded, "No, you are scheduled to orient with the other nurse. Now go and orient with her." I was shocked with their attitude and responses and decided to just orient myself as best as possible. Not a very nice welcome to the p.m. shift.

The medical floor had two sides to the nurse's station, and each of the two nurses had their own side. Thus, the new nurse would have to change sides every time one of the other two nurses had a day off. So even though I might have been taking care of the patients for the past three days and knew their needs, when the one nurse came back, I would have to move to the other side, learn all the new patients, and begin to take care of them until the other nurse came back from her days off and then would have to go back to the other side again. So much for continuity of care. In addition, at the end of the short hallway was the cardiac intensive care unit. Since that unit only had one registered nurse and a licensed vocational nurse on duty, one of us had to relieve the RN for dinner each night. Being the new kid on the block, I was usually the one that was sent back to relieve the RN for dinner break. Knowing very little about cardiac rhythms, I would literally walk around the unit continuously for the thirty minutes that the unit RN was at dinner, making sure every patient was still breathing and praying that none of the patients would develop an irregular rhythm and that no doctor would come into the unit and begin asking questions about the patients. I was so relieved when the RN would finally come back from her dinner break and was very happy to return to my unit.

I loved my job and working with the staff. Working as a nursing assistant at the Reedley Hospital taught me the importance of working together as a team. In Reedley, I had worked with a nurse on the evening shift who had graduated from Stanford University. She would always sit at the desk with her motor board cap and read the paper as my partner and I were running around like chickens with our heads cut off taking care of patients, answering call lights, providing evening care, and making sure that the patients were ready for sleep. She never once offered to help us with our work. It was at that point that I promised myself that I would not be like her and would help the nursing assistants whenever time allowed. I kept my promise during my time of working as a staff nurse often helping the nursing assistants make beds and answer patient's call lights. In turn, whenever I was busy, they would step up to the plate to help me in whichever way they could. We worked as a team, and I also learned from them. Once, when caring for a Filipino man who died and in the process of preparing his body to be picked up by the funeral home, I was taught a lesson in cultural diversity. It was the middle of winter and so it was cold outside. Stepping out of the room to gather some supplies, upon returning, I noticed that the window was open so proceeded to close it. I was then called out to speak to a physician on the phone, and when I returned to the room, the window was open again and upon proceeding to close it again, the Filipino nursing assistant who was working with me informed me that in her culture, they believed that when a person died, they had to open the window in order to allow the spirit to leave the body. Consequently, the window was left open after the explanation.

During this same time, plans for my upcoming wedding were in progress. My sister Esther had volunteered to make my wedding dress and so we would go shopping for material and the items that would be needed to make the dress. My fiancé and I reserved the church and location for the reception, selected our wedding party, the caterer, band, invitations, and made the necessary arrangements for our wedding day. We met with the priest for our wedding instructions and remember him asking us the question, "When do you think you love each other the most?" and we both responded, "Right now," to which he answered, "No, you will love each other the most after you have been married for many years." We both thought this was wrong, but after many years of being married, we both agreed that he was correct. We did indeed love each other more after having been married for many years. I had found my soul mate and was very happy being married.

As mentioned before, coming back home to live was a mistake as my father felt that because I was living at home, he still had a right to tell me what to do even though I was an adult. He was upset with me for not listening to him as to where to get a job; he wanted me to work at the local hospital. If I went out with my fiancé, he wanted me home by 10:00 p.m.; he very much wanted to control me. There was one time when I talked back to him and he began slapping me, and my mother came to my rescue and then he began slapping her. We had to call the sheriff to the house in order to stop him from hitting my mother. It was definitely a mistake to move back home. I was working that evening and was very happy to leave the house. However, the incident definitely affected me and was on my mind while working. Leaving the coffee shop after having dinner, one of my patient's family members tried to get my attention by touching me on my back to ask me a question. I caught myself before almost swinging back and hitting him with my right arm. I was still thinking about being hit by my father. I could not wait to get married in order to be out of his house. My fiancé and I found a one-bedroom furnished apartment in Fresno, which would serve as our first home.

CHAPTER 11
Challenges of Married Life

My fiancé and I got married on August 9, 1969, and had a large wedding, with family and friends attending. Some of my nursing school classmates even attended, and we stayed until all the guests had left. The feeling of freedom came over me as I no longer had to answer my father. We moved into our apartment in Fresno, which was very close to the hospital where I worked. We had not planned where we would go on our honeymoon, and so the next day, we just got into our car and decided to go to Disneyland as neither of us had visited there. We also went to the San Diego Zoo and then traveled along the coast, visiting as many of the missions as we could. We spent the last night of our honeymoon in a beautiful hotel in the Big Sur area overlooking the ocean. We returned home after a week and settled into our apartment as a newlywed couple. Life could not be better.

My husband worked days as a barber, and I was working the p.m. shift. So by the time I would get home at 11:30 or 11:45 p.m., he was already asleep. He was not happy with this arrangement and asked me to get a job working the day shift. I told him that I would ask to be moved to the day shift but that it might be awhile before a position would become available. We were very happy in our small little apartment even though my parents never came to visit us. I felt so free to be able to do the things without having to ask permission from my father. My new husband was very kind and supportive, and basically let me do and go places that I wanted to go. We both worked hard and started planning for a family. In December, I found out I was pregnant with my first child and had a bad case of morning sickness; the p.m. shift was my friend as by the time my shift started, I was no longer nauseated or vomiting.

Our first son, Stephen Joseph, was born on October 4, 1970, and we were both very happy being new parents; a little scared, but very happy. My parents enjoyed being new grandparents, and my brothers and sisters would beg my husband and me to leave Steve with them each time we visited. Even before my son was born, I began having terrible abdominal pains right in the middle of my stomach. At first, I thought it was something that I had eaten or my baby's foot pressing up against my abdomen. The pain would come on in waves, and it became so bad that I finally sought medical help since the pains continued after delivering my baby. After seeing my doctor, he informed me he thought my pains were due to gallstones and referred me to a surgeon. The tests and physical exam by the surgeon confirmed the diagnosis, and I was scheduled for surgery two months after having given birth. The post-operative pain was terrible, and the first time I was asked to get out of bed and walk, it felt like my big abdominal incision was being torn apart. I used all of my strength to get myself out of the bed with the help of my nurse who was my friend and told me that I would not get pneumonia on her shift. So as hard as it was, I got up and walked a short distance.

Since pregnancy at that time was not considered a disability, I had not been receiving a paycheck during my time off after delivery. Now the surgeon was telling me I needed surgery and would have to be off work even longer. I was stressed out thinking that we were going to have to be without a paycheck for an even longer period. However, the surgery would be considered a disability, and thus, I would receive disability pay. Receiving that first paycheck was so wonderful and took away some of our stress so we celebrated with dinner and wine. Since I was going to have to be off work for about two months due to my large abdominal incision, we decided to move from Fresno to a place closer to where my husband was working in Selma, so we began to look for a place to rent. We started by going to a real estate office in Kingsburg. We were greeted by an agent who asked us our last name, and after we both responded, "De La Cruz," he stated, "Oh, isn't that a nice Swedish name." We decided right then and there that we did not want to live in that city. We were able to find a small home in the country which we rented for $75 per month. We knew that we wanted to buy our own home, so when I was able to return to work after the surgery, we decided to try to save the majority of my paycheck for a down payment on a house. Living in the old country house was not a happy time as when I came home from work every afternoon, there were bees flying in the kitchen. I could not wait to get out of that house, and after nine months, we began our search for our first home.

After about a year of working on the medical unit, the German nurse decided that she was taking a three-month leave to go back home. So with her departure, I now had my own side and no longer had to move back and forth from side to side. When the nurse returned from her leave, she quickly informed me that she was back now and so would take her side back; at which point, I informed her that this was no longer her side and that now she would have to bounce back and forth from side to side. I realized then that I was starting to find my voice and use it to make my feelings known. She only stayed on the unit for about a month before she put in for a transfer to another unit.

I had every third weekend off, so we always made plans to go and visit his family and mine. I felt very welcomed by his family but knew that my father did not care for my husband, so it was stressful when we went to visit my family. To my husband's credit, he never complained and always went with me even though my father never really talked to him much. When my sister married her husband, my father liked him very much, and it was very hard for me to watch him talk and joke with my brother-in-law but not with my husband. I could not understand why. I felt that I had done everything right; I had graduated from college, married a Mexican man who was

Catholic, and yet my brother-in-law was Anglo and non-Catholic and got along fine with my father. I was never able to figure it out, but it was painful for me to see and hide the hurt. I told myself not to dwell on it and focused instead on my marriage and work.

I worked very hard and finally was able to move to the day shift after a position had finally become available. While hating to leave my friends on the p.m. shift, it was clear that it needed to happen for the sake of our marriage. I continued to demonstrate my abilities as a nurse and leader, and after three years, was asked to apply for the supervisor position when the current supervisor retired. Not being sure that I was ready to accept the added responsibility, I decided to take the risk. I worked hard to learn my new role and made important changes to the work environment in order to provide supervisory coverage for a longer period of time. The three floor supervisors of the floor changed our schedules so that we would be available to the staff every weekday from 5:00 a.m. to 9:00 p.m. rather than only from 8:00 a.m. to 5:00 p.m. I liked the new responsibilities and was gaining new experiences each and every day.

CHAPTER 12
Facing Discrimination as a Woman

Up until this time, we had been renting and decided that we needed to purchase a home. We began our search and were surprised that some realtors would not consider my nursing income in calculating our total income. We first looked in a new development in the northwest part of Fresno. We found a house plan that we liked, but when they asked about our income, they told us that we would not qualify as they could not consider my income. When I asked why, they told us because I might get pregnant and not work so therefore, they could not consider my income. Consequently, we were denied being able to submit our application on a new home in a new development. Talk about discrimination toward women!

My husband's parents had told us that they would lend us the money for a down payment on a home in Selma which we liked. However, for some unknown reason, they changed their minds and rescinded their offer. We were very disappointed as we had found a house that we liked, but once they took back their offer, we had to decline. We were devastated but did not give up our search.

We finally found a realtor who was willing to work with us and we were able to buy our first home: a three-bedroom, one-bath home in central Fresno. Because my husband was a veteran, we were able to apply for a VA loan which did not require a down payment, but only the closing costs up front. The closing costs were approximately $788, and we barely had enough money in our savings to cover these costs. But it was enough to help us buy our first home. We were very excited to move into our new home but would sometimes lie in bed wondering whether we would be able to make the $165 a month mortgage payment as we had just doubled the amount of money we would be paying for a home. The house had beautiful wood floors but because carpet was the in-thing at the time, we immediately covered all the beautiful wood floors with carpet. Boy, have times changed!

In 1972, I became pregnant with our second child. Jeffrey Alan was born on May 4, 1973. My parents were happy to be grandparents for the second time and both of our sons received much love from their grandparents and aunts and uncles. Since I did not have any morning sickness this time as with my first pregnancy, my assumption was that I was going to have a girl. In trying to prepare our son for the birth of our second child, my husband and I told him that he would be getting a baby sister and her name would be Debra Michelle. To our surprise, we had our second son. Since we were so sure that I was having a girl, we had not discussed any boys' names so when the nurse came to my room to ask me his name, I did not have an answer for her yet. My husband and I asked for a book of boys' names so we could select a name for our new baby. When we just could not decide on a name, I remembered a cowboy actor who had impressed me by the name of Jeff Chandler, so I asked my husband if we could name him Jeffrey and he agreed. One of my doctor friends came by to visit me and asked me, "So what did you name the kid?" and when I responded Jeffrey Alan, he looked puzzled and asked, "Jeffrey Alan De La Cruz? That's like naming my son Poncho Barman!"

When we brought him home and introduced Jeffrey to Stephen, he looked at us with a surprised look on his face and asked, "What happened to Debra Michelle?" A reasonable question from a two and-a-half-year-old. We explained to him that we had brought him a brother instead, and he was happy. As our two sons grew older and if they would have a fight, our older son would often call his brother Debra Michelle just to annoy him.

My husband and I discussed not having more children as my labors had been very long and difficult. While he would have liked to try for a girl, I knew that going through another pregnancy and hard delivery was not an option for me. We decided that I would have a tubal ligation the day after delivery. I was supposed to have our son on May 3 and was scheduled to have a tubal ligation at 10:00 a.m. the following day. However, even after being induced at 9:00 a.m. on the third, Jeff was not born until May 4 at 4:27 a.m. I was only in the maternity ward for a few hours before being whisked off to surgery.

I had saved my sick time at work so that it would be available for me to use after the surgery and therefore receive a paycheck. However, the day before I was to receive my check, I was called by my manager and informed that I would not be receiving a paycheck the next day after all. When I asked why, I was told that because the disability office considered my tubal ligation to be associated with my pregnancy and since they did not recognize pregnancy and giving birth as a disability, I was not eligible to receive payments. Therefore, the hospital could not pay me sick leave until after six weeks post-delivery. Needless to say, we were very disappointed. My husband had decided to go back to college and so was only working part-time now, thus we would not have much of an income for six weeks and would have to live off of our meager savings. Having a new baby was not easy, but we made it. Thank goodness the laws have finally changed, and pregnancy is now considered a disability. I returned to work right after the six weeks as we needed my income. I just could not understand why I could not receive disability pay as I had not had my tubal ligation in the delivery room but had actually gone to the operating room for this surgery. I wrote several letters appealing to the decision to no avail. It did not seem fair that if a man had surgery, he was able to collect disability pay but because I was a woman who had given birth and then later had surgery, I was not eligible for disability pay. It was then that I decided that this was definitely a man's world.

In 1975, we decided that we needed a larger home and so we began our home search again. We found a very nice three-bedroom, two-bath home with a game room in the Hoover High area which we purchased. We were able to sell our first home and used the money as a down payment for our second home. Again, we lay in bed worrying about whether or not we would be able to make the new house payment, now at $364 per month. We had increased our living expenses without increasing our income, so we began to look at our budget to see where we could cut. Since my husband had gone back to college, I thought about going back to working as a staff nurse and switching to the night shift so my husband could watch the boys at night while I was at work and I could watch them during the day, thus eliminating the $150 a month in daycare expenses. When reality set in, we asked ourselves when we would be together as a family if we made this change. We decided that we would cut expenses elsewhere in order for me to continue to work the day shift and keep my position. We became good friends with the realtor who had helped us buy this house, and everything went smoothly with the move. We were very happy there, made some life-long friends, but had dreams of moving to the country to raise our two sons since we had both been raised in the country. After five years of living in this home, we began our search for a home in the country.

Because I was a diploma nurse and did not have a degree, and the fact that I was a minority, I always felt that I had to prove myself to the other nurses and doctors, so I worked twice as hard to excel. I noted that I did not see many minority nurses working at this hospital. There were many minority staff in housekeeping and dietary, but I could count on one hand the number of minority registered nurses. Sometimes doctors would make comments to me about my heritage asking me such questions such as "Where did you go to school, Tijuana Tech?" One evening, I had decided to work the evening shift with my staff and I saw that one of the patient's lights had not been answered promptly so I went to the room to answer it. The patient's doctor was at her bedside and began to tell me that she had complained to him that her light was not being answered in a timely manner. I was trying to ascertain whether it happened more on the day shift, p.m. shift or night shift when the doctor told me, "It is just like the court system, whatever they say goes" to which I responded,

"I don't always agree with the court system."

At that point the doctor said to me, "Then what are you doing in this country, why don't you go back where you came from?"

To which I responded, "Because I am an American citizen, and I have as much right to be here as you do."

I decided that was enough said in front of the patient, so I walked out of the room. He followed me out and told me that he wanted me to go down to administration with him as he was going to report me. I told him that if he felt he needed to report me then he should do it but that I was much too busy to go down and report myself. He did go down and report me to my manager that happened to be in the administrative office at the time. But interestingly enough, after that, every time he would see me in the hallway, he would salute me; not sure why, but he never argued with me again.

While a supervisor, I had the opportunity to apply for an open manager position of one of the medical floors. Unfortunately, I was not selected for the position, and I remember wondering whether it was because I did not have a degree. I believed that I had the ability and skills to become a manager, but I just did not have that piece of paper called a degree. Somedays when times became hectic, I would think of leaving and looking for employment at another facility. However, I would always stop myself for my fear of not being able to get a similar job at the same salary at another facility due to my lack of a degree. I was the primary bread winner and could not afford to take a chance on having to take a cut in pay. One time, my husband and I even looked at purchasing a home on the central coast to get away from the summer heat, but we were held back by my fear of not being able to obtain a supervisory job at one of the facilities on the coast. In a way, I felt stuck.

My being bilingual came in very handy at work as I was able to speak to our monolingual Spanish patients and help meet their needs. I have always been thankful that my parents, in particular my father, made me learn how to speak Spanish; I learned how to write in Spanish in high school. A particular incident that I particularly remember regarding interpretation was helping a physician translate to a seventy-six-year-old Mexican man. The doctor was doing a pulmonary consult and asked me to help him. I gladly went into the patient's room to help. He was asking him simple question about his health, "How long have you been sick? Where do you have pain? What symptoms do you have?" I was doing fine with the interpretation. Then he asked me to ask the man if he had any lumps. Now, my father had never taught me how to say lumps, and I had not learned this word in my Spanish classes, so I was stumped. Wanting to help the doctor, I asked the man the closest thing I felt translated into lumps and ended up asking him, "*Señor, tiene bolas?*"

The patient responded with a huge smile and said, "*Sí, dos.*"

I had just asked him if he had any balls, and he responded, "Yes, two." At that point, I turned red as a beet, and the doctor realizing what I had said told me to ask him if he had any trouble urinating, at which point I responded, "I will not ask him that question," and quickly left the room.

The doctor then went about telling the staff that I had just propositioned a seventy-six-year-old man and everybody laughed. After that, people went about the hospital asking me, "Hey, Pilar, how do you say lumps?"

CHAPTER 13

Introduction to Critical Care

Part of my job as a supervisor was to make sure that we kept the doctors as well as the staff happy. One morning, a pulmonary care doctor came to me complaining that the nurses on the floor did not know how to properly care for his patients with respiratory problems. After letting him vent, I told him that what he needed was to have a special unit where he could train the nurses to care for his patients the way he wanted them cared for and observed. He agreed and left the unit to see his other patients on other units. About an hour after he left the floor, I received a call from the nursing office telling me that the director of nursing wanted to see me. Since it was only 9:30 in the morning, I figured that I could not be in trouble already as it was too early.

I went down to see her and the first thing she told me was, "I understand that you want to start a respiratory intensive care unit," to which I answered with a question, "I do?" She informed me that the doctor who had been complaining had met with her and told her we needed to begin this type of unit and that I was to run it. Much to my surprise, I had just been moved to an intensive care setting. I was sent to an Intensive Care Course that was being given locally by the Area Health Education Center (AHEC) for a three-week intensive training. I would then be sent to do an internship for two weeks at the old San Francisco General Hospital in San Francisco and be mentored by two clinical specialists, one in respiratory and one in cardiac care. I would then come back and open a respiratory intensive care unit as the doctor had requested. I was excited about the opportunity to learn a new type of intensive care nursing. While it was hard leaving my husband and two small children for the two-week period, I was happy that I had been given the opportunity to expand my experience.

I was able to open the unit and hired nurses and trained them in respiratory intensive care. I was working long hours but really enjoyed the experience. I remember having to suction my first patient through his endotracheal tube and worrying that I was killing him when he turned blue as I was suctioning him. I soon realized that this happens, and it was a normal response. Because we were very short of nurses, as the supervisor, I sometimes had to work a double shift if the nurse called in sick and no one else could come in to work the shift. So I would work sixteen hours in a row, but I loved the work. Since respiratory intensive care medicine was a new specialty, several of the doctors who admitted patients to this unit were not familiar with ventilator settings and other treatment modalities. I was fortunate to work with wonderful respiratory therapists who were the experts in this field. I remember telling Sylvia, the manager of the department, that I would teach her everything I knew about respiratory nursing if she would teach me about the ventilators. She agreed, and we developed a great working relationship and friendship.

Having this new knowledge, I had to put it to work quickly. We had a patient who had chronic obstructive pulmonary disease (COPD) and was on oxygen at two liters. He was rather drowsy, and it was hard to awaken him. After discussing the situation with the respiratory therapist, we both decided that the patient was receiving too much oxygen, but in order to determine whether this assumption was correct, we needed to have a set of blood gasses. I proceeded to call his physician, a very good internal medicine physician who could be rather difficult. I called him and gave him our assumption. His response was, "What you really want me to do is to order blood gasses," and I responded yes.

He then told me, "I will be in to see him this evening on my rounds and then I will decide whether or not he needs blood gasses, but in the meantime, take good care of my patient."

Since it was time for me to go off duty, I reported my assessment of this patient to the oncoming nurse and told her that I would call her later to find out what had happened with this patient. I called back around eight o'clock in the evening, and sure enough, the doctor had been in, ordered blood gasses, and his level of carbon dioxide was too high, so he lowered the oxygen level to one liter instead of two.

The next morning, when I saw the patient's physician come onto the unit, I wanted to say, "I told you so," but I held my tongue and just said good morning. But then he came by and found me and told me, "You know, you were right yesterday. He was receiving too much oxygen, so I lowered it." I told him that I felt uncomfortable questioning his order, and he told me to never be afraid to question his order. After that, whenever there was a respiratory problem with one of his patients, he would consult with me if needed, even to the point of letting me write the orders for the setup of a ventilator and then he would review them and sign the order.

One of my most challenging patients was an elderly woman who asked her husband to go to the store and buy her some Drano. Her husband went to the store and returned with the granule type of the product. The wife informed him that he had bought the wrong product, told him she wanted the liquid form, and sent him back to the store. The husband did as she requested, and when he brought her the liquid Drano, she proceeded to drink it as a way of committing suicide. The husband had no idea that she wanted to take her life. Unfortunately for her, the liquid drain cleaner did not kill her right away. She was in our Respiratory Intensive Care Unit for one week as we were suctioning sloughing tissue from her esophagus and stomach. She suffered a terrible death, and it was very hard for us to watch as she finally got her wish of ending her life.

Another challenge we had was a sixteen-year-old African American girl with status asthmaticus. She had been placed on a ventilator but was fighting the ventilator so was not receiving the benefit of the ventilation due to her restlessness. I had just read an article about the use of Pavulon, a medication used for patients who were fighting the ventilator and not receiving the benefit of artificial ventilation. This drug actually paralyzed the lungs, thus allowing the ventilator to work effectively and helping to oxygenate the patient. I mentioned it to her doctor as nothing we were doing was helping her and we felt we were going to lose her if we did not do something. He asked me if I had the article with me, and I told him I had it in my locker. He asked me to get it so I ran down to my locker and brought him the article. After reading it, he asked me if I was willing to try it, knowing that we would have to keep her completely sedated while she was receiving the medication. We decided to go ahead, and this drug literally saved her life. She was able to eventually be removed from the ventilator and be discharged home. A real success story. I had fallen in love with respiratory intensive care nursing and was viewed as an expert in this type of nursing.

One Sunday morning when I reported to work in the unit, I was informed that we had a one-and-a-half-year-old as a patient. I immediately requested to have a pediatric nurse work with us as we were not familiar with pediatric medication doses or normal vital sign ranges for children. The little boy just did not look good, but since he had a tracheostomy in place, he could not cry, but I knew something was wrong. A call was placed to the surgeon who was the patient's doctor and shared with him the concerns about the child. He was impatient with me and told me, "Just get a nurse in there that knows how to suction him," and hung up the phone. I guess my call had disturbed his Sunday morning routine.

At last, the child's pediatrician came in to check on him, and I asked him if he would order an x-ray on the child as he seemed to be having trouble breathing. He was very nice and ordered the x-ray. A portable chest x-ray was done, and a few minutes later, I received a call from the radiologist who had read the x-ray. He informed me that the child has a bilateral pneumothorax (both lungs were collapsing), and if we did not do something quick, we would lose the child. I quickly called the surgeon and prepared the equipment that would be needed to insert chest tubes into the child to re-expand the lungs. It was a frightening experience, but I was able to keep my cool, had all the equipment that the surgeon would need for the procedure, and waited for him to arrive, which he did shortly. I also wanted to tell him, "I told you so," but again held my tongue and was just happy that we had been able to save the child.

Unfortunately, after about a year of opening the unit, my husband and I were riding our bicycles with our children when I hit the back of a parked truck on my street and fell off my bicycle with my youngest son riding behind me. I was embarrassed as small children also riding their bikes asked if I was okay. To prove that I was all right, I got back up on my bike and rode home. I had pain in my leg all night, and the next morning decided to go to the emergency department and be examined. The orthopedist on call came to see me and informed me after looking at my x-rays that I had fractured my right fibula. He told me that he did not have to put it in a cast but that I would have to be off work for six weeks. I protested and told him I had to work as we did not have enough nurses, so I could not afford to be off of work. After hearing different reasons why I could not be off work for six weeks, he became exasperated with me and told me, "Read my lips, Pilar. You are going to have to be off work for six weeks." Due to the fact that we did not have enough nurses, the unit had to be closed for a period of time until I returned to work.

Once I returned to work and reopened the unit, I began to notice the problems of having three different units on different floors with three different nurse managers. I suggested to my director of nursing that it would make sense to combine all three units under one manager as this would promote cross-training of the nurses and allow for greater flexibility with staffing. She dismissed my idea, telling me that the doctors would never go for that change. I supported her decision but still felt that it made sense. About six months later, she brought her friend, a registered nurse from Los Angeles, and appointed her to the position of manager of all three units. I guess my idea finally made sense to her. I was upset that while it had been my idea, I was not given the opportunity to become the manager, but she convinced me that the new person she had hired had many years of experience as an ICU nurse and would do a great job. I respected her decision and told myself that I would help support the new manager. I remained as the supervisor of the respiratory intensive care unit. After about a year of her leadership, it became obvious to all of the nurses that she did not know as much as she claimed to know about intensive care nursing. She was making administrative decisions that just did not make sense, which caused problems for the nurses. Nurses who were unhappy with her leadership began to complain, and several actually left the hospital. I tried to help her, but she would not listen to my suggestions. As she began to realize that she was in trouble, she saw me in the hallway one day and told me, "You know, Pilar, I may fail at this job, but if I do, I will take you down with me." I did not tell her anything, but to myself I said, "No way, lady."

As more and more nurses threatened to leave, the doctors became upset and complained to the director. She finally had to face the fact that her friend could not do the job, and she let her go. I was then called to her office and given the job as the manager of all three intensive care units. The nurses and doctors were happy and things got back to normal. I worked very hard in my new position, made positive changes, and the nurses were happy again. We were able to recruit new nurses, and a few of the nurses who had left decided to come back once the change was made. We began to cross-train the nurses, and while they were not happy at first, they soon realized how the cross-training would actually make them better nurses and provide them with greater flexibility, security, and job opportunities.

We were on the merit system for our annual evaluations. The goal was to recognize the accomplishments of the individual person and reward them based on their performance over the past year. The evaluation scale went from 0–6 percent. When I was called to the director's office for my evaluation, I was told that I had done a great job this past year and I really deserved a 6 percent but that if I was given a 6 percent I would be making more money than a few of the managers who had been in the position longer than I had been so she was going to give me a 3 percent. I thanked her without complaining, trying to convince myself that I should be happy with a 3 percent that I had been given. I had not yet learned the importance of being assertive. So much for performance-based evaluations. I told myself later that I would never let this happen to me again.

I was the mother of two small boys who needed much attention. My husband was finishing his degree at Fresno State, we had just bought a new home and life was stressful. I was having to put in many hours at work and was not getting enough sleep. My husband and I were struggling to raise two boys and keep up with their activities and needs. Finally, the straw came that broke the camel's back. I was getting ready to bake a coffee cake to take to the scheduled staff meeting I had planned for the night shift at 4:30 a.m. the next day. When I tried to get the brown sugar out of the box, it had hardened, and I could not use it. I began to cry and started to bang the box on the kitchen counter. My husband heard the commotion and came into the kitchen to see what was happening.

When he saw my condition, he just wrapped his arms around me and held me and told me it was going to be okay. I made the decision that night that the manager's job was just too stressful for me at this time, and I would have to make a choice to either save my marriage or my job. I decided that my marriage was more important, so the next day, I gave my letter of resignation after being in the position for almost two years. While working as the manager, I had taken and passed the national critical care exam which certified me as a Critical Care Registered Nurse (CCRN). I was one of the first two nurses in the hospital to achieve this status. Because of my certification, I was able to take a job in the Education Department serving as a clinical instructor for critical care.

This job was much less stressful, and I vowed that I would never again accept another management/supervision position. I loved my time working in the education department. I worked with some wonderful and very talented nurses in the department, and our reputation for being an excellent department was well-known throughout the Central Valley. We had a manager who believed in our talents and touted our knowledge and talents to administrators. We all loved working for her; she became one of my mentors. I thought I had died and gone to heaven working in this department. I was able to establish our own critical care course to train new nurses and offer other educational classes for the staff. Even though I had to take a cut in pay with this move, I was having fun and enjoying my work again, which was much less stressful.

Baby Picture, 1 year old, 1947.

High School graduation picture, Reedley High School, Class of '64.

Rocky, the Alaskan Huskie dog belonging to the nuns, Sisters of Charity who ran the hospital and nursing school.

Me and my friend, and nurse colleague, celebrating receiving my master's degree.

O'Connor School of Nursing, graduation picture, 1968.

My first car, 1969 Pontiac Firebird, 6-cylinder, overhead cam.

First husband, Joe, and me in Hawaii, 1980.

On vacation in Southern California, 1982 (Joe, me, Stephen and Jeffrey).

Mother and Father, Joe and Margaret Ybarra, 1991, Salinas, CA.

Family picture, 1991, two months before losing our mother to cancer (front row: nephew Russell, nephew Justin, mother, nieces Lindsey, Nicole and Sarah, father, nephew Michael and son Jeff; second row, brother Eddie, niece Amy, nephew Jason, sister-in-law Lou, brother Jess, sister Esther, brother-in-law Mickey, sister Mattie, me, picture of my son Steve who was away at college, first husband Joe, sister Terri and brother-in-law Jim).

50th birthday party celebration with Uncle Ben, Aunt Isabel and cousins Cecilia and Alice Ybarra.

Making tamales at Christmas time with family (nieces Sarah and Amy and brother Jess and sister-in-law Lou).

With brothers and sisters in Salinas, 1997 (brother Jess, sisters Terri, Mattie and Esther, me and little brother Eddie).

Long time friends, Ana and Carlos Medrano who accompanied me to Boise, Idaho for my presentation after Joe's death.

With high school friends (Ana, Mary, Sally, Isabel and me at one of our monthly lunches).

On vacation in Newport News, VA 2000.

Family picture while vacationing in Cabo San Lucas, 2014 (pictured are son Stephen, daughter-in-law Barbara, me, me and my good nurse friend, Carolyn granddaughter Breanna, my second husband Felix, granddaughter Gracie, son Jeffrey and daughter-in-law Alisha).

With my grandson, Adrian (AJ), at his kindergarten graduation, 2017.

Sister weekend in San Luis Obispo, 2018.

Wedding day, May 2018 to David Samoulian in our backyard.

CHAPTER 14
Challenges of Country Living

About this time, we intensified our search for a home in the country. My husband had been saving his Cal-Vet loan application until we found a country home. After looking both on the west and east side of Fresno, we decided to settle on the east side due to the view and water availability. We found a new home that had been built as a spec home in the Sanger area. We had seen it being built as we would drive out in the country on our way to visit our parents. The new home was located on two acres and was larger than our current home, with room to grow. We called the listing agent and asked to see the home. He met us on a Sunday afternoon and showed us the property, and we both fell in love with the home. As we were leaving, the realtor said to us, "I don't think you can afford to buy this house." We wondered why he would make such a comment but did not respond and discussed his comment once we were in the car. My husband said to me in a determined voice, "I am going to buy you this house."

    We decided to call our realtor friend who had sold us our second home and asked him if he would help us put an offer in on this home. He agreed and so we put in our offer in February 1980, and our friend called the listing agent. The next morning, the listing agent called me, rather upset, and asked me why we had called the other realty agent. I responded to him, "Because we don't trust you after the comment you made to us." He was not happy, but we were looking out for our interests. The asking price was $118,000, and after discussing this with our realtor friend, we decided to make an offer of $101,500. The interest rates were high, and we knew that the house had been on the market for almost a year. Consequently, they decided to accept our offer, and we signed a contract for a sixty-day escrow period. We were trading our current home as a down payment and had a few repairs to make which we did. We gave a down payment and started escrow.

We were excited about moving to our home in the country and began to make plans for our move. I was at a critical care conference in Atlanta when my husband called me and told me that the builder had called him and told him that the deal was off. I could not understand why as we had done everything that we had agreed to do for our current home and felt we had a valid contract. When I returned home the next day, we called our realtor friend and told him what had happened. He said that we had a valid contract, and they could not just pull the rug from under our feet. We tried talking with the builder and realtor, but they would not budge, and actually put the house back on the market. I shared an office with my friend at work, and after telling her what had happened, she agreed to call the listing agent and pretend to be an interested buyer. Since we shared an office, she would put the phone on speaker, and I was able to hear their entire conversation. She asked if there were any offers on the house and was told that there had been one but that the party had not qualified; we both knew this was not true. I decided to begin to write letters to the Real Estate Board and Better Business Bureau complaining about the listing agency. This went on for weeks, and I was getting ready to write a letter to the US Department of Housing and Urban Development (HUD) to complain about these actions, and our realtor friend informed the seller about what I was about to do. The seller and listing realtor finally consented to honor the original contract, but it took until the end of July for this to take place. After we had made our offer, the interests' rates had dropped and they realized that they had sold the house at too low a price and wanted to correct that, so they decided to try to sell the house again to another buyer.

Before we actually moved into our new house, I was visiting the house one day and found small piles of what looked like sawdust on the kitchen floor. I notified the seller of this, and they found out that green wood had been used to build the kitchen cabinets and the wood had beetles in it. So the seller had to drape the entire house and fumigate it. The house needed to be painted before the bank would loan us the money on the house, so my husband and I spent one entire weekend painting the sides and back of the house (the front was redwood) so that we could obtain our loan. The construction people had also left a pile of construction odds and ends in the backyard, and we also had to dispose of all of that junk. The house was surrounded by tall weeds that we had to take care of as it was considered a fire hazard. After it was all over and we were safely in our home, the seller and listing realtor met with us to make sure everything was in order and apologized for the problems. I informed the listing realtor that he and the seller had picked on the wrong Mexicans.

We were told when we made our offer that the house had a construction loan on it and that a balloon payment would be due in April of 1981. We were okay with this as we had applied for our Cal-Vet loan and figured it would come through before then. In September, the seller informed us that he had given us the incorrect time frame and that the balloon payment was actually due in October of that year. The balance due on the house was $80,000. Because Cal-Vet only loaned a maximum of $55,000, we had to come up with the additional $25,000. My parents had agreed to loan us the difference, and my mother went to her bank to have the money transferred to our bank account. When I went to the bank to get the money, they told me that since the money had not reached their bank yet, they could not give me a check. They knew that the money had been deposited, but their bank had not yet received the transfer. I asked to speak to the branch manager and explained the situation and that we needed to close that day. I told him that if they did not give me the check that I was going to sit in front of their front door until they did. He agreed to give me the money, and we were finally able to close on our house.

My father bought each of our sons a goat so that they could eat all the grass that surrounded the house as it was a house and weeds. They goats were a pain, and they ate everything in sight including grass. They also ate the tree that we had planted as our first tree for our house. Eventually, both of the goats died, and we did not have to worry about them anymore. We hired someone to come and disk all of the weeds.

Our sons were both interested in sports—soccer, baseball, basketball—so on weekends and during the week after work, I became a taxi taking them to their practices and games. One son played soccer games in Fresno and the other played in Sanger, and they both had games on Saturday; sometimes around the same time. Consequently, I would have to go back and forth, and sometimes had to make plans with other parents and ask for help to take one of my sons to their game and then I would get there as soon as I could. Since my husband worked on Saturdays, I was responsible for getting them to their events on Saturday. I remember my mother getting upset with me one day and telling me that I should be resting on Saturday rather than running around taking them to their games. She knew how hard I worked during the week and was concerned about my health. I told her that someday I would have plenty of time to rest, but that right now, it was their time and I had to make sacrifices to support them in their interests. When I was later asked why I had waited so long to go back to school to obtain my degree, I responded that I wanted to make sure that I had time for my sons and be able to be at their events. I remembered how important that had been to me and the promise that I had made to myself. I was exhausted from working full-time and from supporting all of our sons' activities, but I knew things would get better as they grew older.

CHAPTER 15
Return to Management

After a few years of working in the Education Department, the current supervisor decided to accept a supervisory position on one of the clinical units and left our department. The manager called me into her office and asked me to take on the supervisory job for the department. I told her that I was not interested, that I had sworn that I would never go back into a management position again. After continued pressure from the manager to take the position, I relented, and I shared the position with another nurse. I was responsible for the clinical instructors, and the other supervisor was responsible for continuing education. In my role, I was required to attend the nurse manager meetings every week to identify any educational needs of the nursing staff and then work to meet those needs. A new director of nursing had been brought on board and after working with her for a year, she asked me to take on the position of manager of the critical care and telemetry units. I told her I was not interested as I was very happy working in the Education Department. She would not take no for an answer and kept after me every time she saw me. I finally relented and agreed to take on the position with the caveat that I would be able to take off early two days a week, without feeling guilty, to go to my son's soccer games which were held twice a week at 3:00 p.m. When she approved my request, I accepted the position. I guess that the moral of this story is to never say never.

I began my new job as a manager and was actually excited about the new opportunity. There was no training for the position that was offered at the time. My first day in my new position, while sitting at my desk in my office I asked myself what my role was, and the response was manager. Manager of what? The response was manager of people. So after realizing that my role was a manager of people, I told myself if that was my role, then this new manager better get out of her office and be with the staff that I was to manage, as I could not do that by sitting behind a desk. Thus began my transformation of becoming a manager who learned the value of MBWA, management by walking around and talking to the staff. I made rounds every day, and the staff knew that if they did not see me, it meant that I was not at work that day. I found that by being out with the staff, the communication and interaction was better as I was available to them if they had a question or concern. I could see for myself any issues they were having to deal with regarding equipment or policy issues, and they could always stop and ask me a question. This type of management worked for me, and I used it throughout the rest of my career.

One of the challenges in this role was not having a sufficient number of nurses. We were often short, and nurses were having to work overtime to cover shifts. Part of my job was to do the schedules for the nurses every six weeks. This job was especially difficult during the holiday season—Thanksgiving, Christmas Eve, Christmas Day, New Year's Eve, and New Year's Day. The nurses were asked to sign up for their first, second, and third choice, and every effort was made to give them their requested choice if at all possible. I would even allow them to split Christmas Day by splitting the shift with another nurse. A nurse with small children would ask to be off the first part of the shift so she could be home with her kids on Christmas morning and work the second part of the shift. As long as the shift was covered, I was happy. One year, I had taken the schedules home with me to finalize them in the evening, and the next morning as I was crossing the busy street, they accidently fell out of my hands and scattered in the middle of the street. I asked myself the question whether I would rather take my chances with the ICU nurses or with the cars. My decision came quick and soon

BUT I WANT TO BE A NURSE

I was standing in the middle of the street waving my arms to get the cars to stop. I had decided I would rather take my chances with the cars than with the ICU staff. So I stood in the middle of the street and waved my hands getting the cars to stop until I was able to pick up all the schedules before they were all torn up and ruined.

Along with being short of nurses, we would run out of equipment and supplies needed, and the nurses were having to do non-nursing jobs in order to keep the unit running. The unions were actively trying to organize the nurses in Fresno and a couple of nurses in the ICU decided to form a group of nurses who were not interested in joining a union but who wanted to see things get better. I would have meetings with them and tried to meet their needs, but they wanted to meet with the director of nursing and share their feelings directly with her. I arranged for the meeting with her to allow them to vent their frustrations. A meeting took place and the nurses took turns explaining their frustrations to the director. I could see the director's face becoming redder as they presented their concerns. They did not want a union but wanted to be heard. After the meeting, the director asked me to come to her office. I knew she was not happy with the outcome of the meeting. She directed me to fire the two nurses who were the spokespersons for the group. I asked her on what grounds as in my opinion, they had not done anything wrong, and they were both good nurses. She said they were troublemakers and were going to cause trouble. I told her that we had no grounds to fire them; they had just expressed their frustrations and wanted to see some changes made to improve their working conditions. She insisted that they be fired, and I told her that I would not do that. I warned her that we did not have a union yet, but if we fired the two nurses, I could guarantee her that we would get a union as the other nurses would take up their cause. She told me that it was either them or me. I responded that it would have to be me as I was not willing to fire them and left her office truly expecting to be fired for insubordination.

As it so happened, she was asked to leave a few days later by the Chief Operating Officer, and I continued on in my role. I was not happy that she was gone but glad that I had stood my ground and done the right thing in not firing the two nurses. While never sharing this story with the nurses, they were smart and able to figure out what had happened. This situation was only one of the many challenges faced as a manager.

We had started an open-heart program, and the cardiac surgeon was known for his yelling when he was unhappy with something. He would often come into my office and yell and could be heard all the way down the hall. He was a very good surgeon and was always buying food for the nurses on the weekends to try to make up for his yelling.

One day, we made a bet on a TV program and the deal was that whoever lost the bet would have to take the other one to lunch. I lost the bet, so the next time I saw him, I asked him where he wanted to go to lunch. His response was, "Harris Ranch." Now this restaurant is located in Coalinga, a town at least one hour away from Fresno, and so I told him that we did not have time to go to Harris Ranch for lunch. He disagreed and told me to meet him at the airport. I was not aware that he owned a plane and also flew his own plane. So my two supervisors and I met him at the airport, boarded his plane, and off we went to Harris Ranch. This was my first time flying in a small plane so it was a new experience. We had a great lunch, and he insisted on paying for it. We flew back and went back to work.

On another occasion, he decided that he wanted me to learn how to ski, as I had never learned before, so he invited me and my two supervisors up to his condo in North Shore at Lake Tahoe where we went to Squaw Valley to ski. He paid for me to have private lessons in the morning, and I tried to bribe my instructor by giving her money if she would just let me go to the coffee shop and drink coffee and tell him that I took the lessons, but alas, she would not go for this option. So I struggled, falling more times than I care to remember. In the afternoon, he became my instructor. He asked me to ski toward him and since I did not know how to turn yet, I skied right over his brand-new skis. He then decided that we were going to go on the chair lift and go up to the top of the mountain. Well, since I had not done this before, I could not get up on the chair. My skis kept sliding in the mushy snow, and after much trying to get up in the chair, my head was where my butt should have been and I kept sliding. He just sat there pretending he did not know me. By the time I was finally able to be pulled up by the attendant, there was a very long line of people waiting to get on chair lift. I was relieved to finally be sitting on the chair lift but soon realized that I would have to get off of it.

He told me, "Whatever you do, don't fall, as you will embarrass me." Of course, when getting off the chair lift, I immediately fell. I managed to get myself up, but I kept falling.

I finally got frustrated and yelled, "I quit!" to which he responded, "Pilar, I have known you for sixteen years, and you have never been a quitter and you are not going to start now. So get up off your butt and start skiing."

After falling for what seemed like the one hundredth time, he told me that the resort closed the hill at 4:00 p.m. and that they were going to have to send the St. Bernard dogs to look for us. Since it was only 3:00 p.m., I figured we still had an hour and tried a new tactic. Every time I fell down, I would roll as far as possible and then would get up and try again. After much falling and effort, I was finally able to ski down the mountain. We both collapsed when we reached the bottom. I swore off skiing ever again, but the next morning, we went back to the mountain, and I was able to ski. However, this experience told me that skiing was not my sport. He later told me that he was sure that if we would have recorded my ski experience and submitted it to the TV show, *America's Funniest*

Home Movies, that we could have won the $10,000 prize; he was probably right.

Our open-heart program grew and made good money for the hospital, and the challenge was having enough open-heart nurses to care for his patients. Sometimes, he would do three cases in one day, which really strained our resources. Another cardiac surgeon who had started the open-heart program at Children's Hospital decided to join our team. He had been working at Community's main competitor hospital and decided to expand his services to our hospital. He was very particular, and one day, he came to my office and informed me that he only wanted certain open-heart nurses taking care of his patients. I let him express his views and then informed him that he could not make that request as all of the designated open-heart nurses had been equally trained and would all take turns taking care of his patients just like they did for the other surgeon. I let him know that if he had a problem with the care delivered by one of the nurses, then he should come and talk to me. He did not argue, got out of his chair, and left my office. I never received a complaint from him on any one of the open-heart nurses.

Our nurses all worked twelve-hour shifts, and because we were short of nurses, the nurses who worked the day shift would have to take turns and rotate to the night shift to cover every other month. One of our open-heart nurses had returned to school to obtain her master's degree in order to become a family nurse practitioner. Because of her classes, she changed from working full-time to *per diem* status as she could not rotate between the day and night shifts due to her classes. However, she did work the seven shifts a pay period like the full-time nurses, and during her vacation times (summer and Christmas), she would work the night shifts.

We had instituted a new policy to give recognition to critical care nurses who successfully passed the national critical care exam and became certified as CCRNs. A bonus of $2625 was given to these nurses, and the policy stated that they had to work full-time, which was considered to be seven twelve-hour shifts in a two-week period. I submitted all of the eligible nurses' names to Human Resources (HR) so that they could receive their bonuses. However, the HR director refused to pay the open-heart nurse who was working *per diem* due to her school schedule, stating that the policy stated that the nurses had to be working full-time and she was listed as *per diem*. I tried my best to help the HR director understand that this nurse was indeed working the schedule of a full-time nurse and deserved to receive the bonus, but he denied my repeated requests. He was concerned that other nurses might also have a similar request and what would we do then. I told him we would have to look at each individual case and do what made sense. After learning that the nurse was thinking of leaving and going to work for the competing hospital who would pay her for her CCRN, I decided to play hardball. I met with the HR director again and told him, "I am tired of trying to convince you to do the right thing, so don't pay her the bonus and let her leave to go to our competitor. However, when the cardiac surgeon comes yelling at me because he cannot do his open-heart case due to a lack of nurses, I am going to bring him to your office, and you can explain to him why you allowed not only a critical care nurse, but a trained open-heart nurse to leave for $2,625."

He finally said to me, "Okay, you can pay her," and I said thank you and walked out the door. We were able to keep this nurse. Talk about being penny wise and pound foolish, his way of thinking made no sense whatsoever.

I had the opportunity to work with some very good nursing managers; we worked hard but also had fun. We were all dedicated to ensuring that the hospital was successful. On occasion, my style of management was different than theirs, and I was called on it by my boss. I remember one situation where the four supervisors who reported to me would get behind on their employee evaluations.

Each supervisor had fifty to sixty employees reporting to them, and while they tried to keep up with the evaluations, they were constantly being interrupted by situations happening on the unit, thus the evaluations did not get completed. We decided to implement a policy within our group of giving each one of them a paper day once a month, where they could stay home and work on them so that they could keep up with their employee evaluations. The other three would take turns covering the unit for the supervisor on a paper day. The assistant director of nursing called me into her office one day as the other managers had complained that I was allowing the four supervisors who reported to me to take a paper day. I told her that they were taking the day to catch up on their employee evaluations, and they could not do that at work due to constant interruptions by staff if they were in the hospital, so I would let them do their evaluations at home.

She asked me, "How do you know they are actually working at home?"

I responded that I would have a stack of evaluations sitting on my desk for review and my signature after their paper day; I was an outcomes person and not a process person. I continued with this practice. One of the managers used to call me the "little Mexican girl;" she said she was teasing, but I was never quite sure and just played along with it.

A new director of nursing was hired, and after she had been with the organization for a year, she called me to her office and told me she wanted me to take over the management of the Emergency Department (ER).

"No, not the emergency department," I protested. "I don't know anything about ER."

This went on for a few weeks as I really did not want to take over this new department. I had never worked in the ER like the current manager and knew it would not be easy. She told me that I had the management skills that were needed to manage this struggling department. The current manager had a very good relationship with the Emergency Room physicians and staff and common sense told me that I would be walking into a hostile environment with them. The staff and the physicians would think that I had asked that the manager be removed in order to get the position. I found out later that this was indeed the case and even some of the secretaries in the nursing office thought this was true. Little did they know how much I had protested this action. I was able to take over the management of the department and began to make positive changes like obtaining the necessary equipment that they had needed for some time and had not been able to secure. It did not take long for the staff to realize that I was moving the department in the right direction, and they began to trust me and work with me to move forward. After much hard work, I was able to earn the respect of both the Emergency Room doctors and staff. I was invited to be part of their celebrations, and we became a team.

A fond memory of my work with the ER department occurred on a weekend when I was the manager-on-duty covering the house. I was called by the ER unit clerk who invited me to come down and have some rum cake that one of the staff members had made and brought into the department to share. When I finally was able to take a break, I walked into the Emergency Department, and in the hallway, I could smell the rum. I asked the nurse who had made the cake if she had added the rum to the mix before it was baked or afterward.

She informed me that she had poured it over the cake once it was baked. I told the staff to please get rid of the cake before we all got fired for having alcohol on the unit. No one was happy about having to throw out the cake, but we all kept our jobs.

CHAPTER 16

A Change Is Coming

Our corporation was struggling financially, and a consultant group was called in by the doctors and Board of Trustees. After many meetings with doctors and management, the end result was that our long-term CEO was fired, and the head of the consulting group became our new CEO. A notice was sent out to all employees informing us that we would all have to reapply for our jobs as there were new expectations. Many of the people who had been in management and supervisory positions lost their jobs, and everything was in an uproar. One of my physician friends later said to me, "We did not want staff to lose their jobs, all we wanted was a change in the CEO position; we never wanted anything to happen to the staff."

I could not believe his thinking and I asked him, "If you think you have termites in your kitchen and you call a pest control company to come and check out your kitchen for termites, do you think they are only going to look at the kitchen?" He could not answer me and walked off.

A new administrative team was brought in, and many changes were made. Our team of eight nursing managers was informed that we had all lost our jobs and that there would now be three director of nursing positions and that those individuals would come from the current eight managers. We would all have to apply for these three positions and a decision would be made as to who would be the new leaders for the nursing department. We were informed on Friday morning and were told that they needed our answer by the next Monday; not much time for such a crucial decision.

As you can imagine, we were all in shock and angry at the same time. We decided to get together at one of the managers' home on Saturday morning. At first, we decided that none of us should apply, but when we came back to our senses, we realized that it would not look good if none of us applied, so in the end, all but two of us decided to apply for the three positions. One decided to go back to staff, and one accepted a position running the employee health department. I applied for one of the three positions but was not expecting to be appointed as I did not have a degree, which was preferred, and I had just gone back to school two years earlier to obtain my bachelor's degree in nursing. All these past years, I had been promoted due to my abilities, but now, I would be expected to have a degree. I was still eighteen months away from completing the program. All of the other managers all had a bachelor's degree, and one had her masters and one other one was just a few of months away from completing her master's degree.

When the day finally arrived to announce the three new directors, I was surprised to be named one of the three. However, the appointment required that I complete my bachelor's degree within three years in order to keep my position. When asked why I had waited so long to get my degree, my response was that I had two sons who were very active with their school activities and sports; they were my priority, and so my goal was to return to school once they were older. I never regretted that decision.

Sometimes a guilty feeling would come over me as I realized I was actually jealous of my husband who had the opportunity to get his bachelor's degree under the GI Bill and was not even using it in his work. Under his GI Bill, he attended both Fresno City College and Fresno State University. He had planned to major in computer science but had changed majors when it became too difficult for him. He decided to pursue a Spanish major and graduated with a Bachelor of Arts degree in humanities. He then decided he did not want to teach and instead accepted a job as an insurance agent selling life insurance. I knew that he did not have the personality for this type of job but supported him in his decision. After six months of working with a company, he was let go and began his search for another job. He was hired by another company, this time as an insurance adjuster with a large firm. He had to travel to Atlanta, Georgia, for training at the home office for six weeks and then came back home and began to work in the local office. He seemed to like it at first and did well for about nine months, but then he was not able to keep up with the demands of the job and was let go from that job as well. When he finally confessed to me that he had been let go, he tried looking for another similar job with no success. In desperation, he found a job with a friend who had a janitorial business. I knew he was not happy doing that job as it was an evening job and interfered with us being together as a family for dinner and attending his son's sports events.

When we finally sat down to discuss his future, he told me what he really enjoyed doing was being a barber, so we decided that he should go back to barbering, but this time, he should buy his own shop and work for himself. So he bought out a barber business and went back to work as a barber and was happy again; so much for that bachelor's degree which I so desperately wanted.

Our director of nursing was from New York so she would say things the way she saw it, which did not always go over well with administrative staff. She introduced some new concepts to the nursing department and was making some headway with changing the culture. She decided to travel to England to celebrate the one hundredth birthday of Florence Nightingale, and she took a couple of staff with her. They visited the museum as well as the gravesite and brought back valuable information that they were able to share with the rest of us. While there, she shopped for some china that she put on her hospital credit card instead of her own personal card. When she submitted her expenses, the china expenses along with the business expenses were submitted for payment—by mistake according to her—and when this was discovered, she was fired. I had enjoyed working for her and was sad to see her leave, but the other managers did not feel the same way.

After a short period of time, the recruitment for a new director of nursing was launched and a nurse executive from the Midwest came onboard. After six months of being in the position, the three of us directors had the opportunity to go on a retreat with her and had a facilitator who informed her that she was only communicating with one of the directors and the other two felt left out. She did not accept that well, but we moved forward. However, through her actions, it became very clear to me that she did not think I knew much since I did not have a degree. When I would go down to her office to speak with her, she would not pay attention to what I was saying, instead she would be looking out the window. She worked closely with the two directors who had their degrees and basically ignored me. I felt discriminated against but knew it would not do me any good to complain. Initially, the one director who had her master's degree for some time seemed to feel that she was better than me. She seemed to have the ear of the chief nurse and got the attention. When she was asked by one of my friends what it was like being a new director, she informed her that it was difficult when working with uneducated people referring mainly to me. I never forgot this comment, and she lost my respect. Eventually, she left nursing and became a hair stylist.

I knew I had to get out of this situation and looked for other leadership opportunities within the organization. When I went to Human Resources to speak with the nurse recruiter to ask her what was available she advised me that the only management position available was for a clinical director of the new subacute unit that was to open soon. It was going to be run by an outside management company, and they were looking to hire a clinical director, but they wanted the director to be their employee. I was not interested in giving up my years of seniority to go and work for an unknown company, but I was asked to send them my curriculum vitae anyway. I faxed it to the company, and thirty minutes later they called me back and informed me that they were interested in hiring me and I could remain as an employee of the hospital. I decided to accept the position and gave the director of nursing my notice. I believe she felt she had done her job in getting rid of me.

The clinical director position would report to the administrator of a sister hospital as well as to the president of the management company. When I talked with the hospital administrator of the sister hospital about the position, he told me that I would be reporting to two bosses and either one could decide that I was not doing the job to their satisfaction and fire me. I understood that this was a risk but felt I was going into this job with my eyes open. He quoted me a salary that was unacceptable to me as it was almost at the level of a new supervisor salary and I had many years of nursing management experience. Again, I sensed discrimination as he knew my situation and was trying to pay me as little as possible. Taking a deep breath, I responded that I would not take the position for the salary he was offering as we both knew that my years of management experience was worth more than he was offering as a starting salary. I had finally learned how to become assertive. I was taking a risk but felt confident in my decision and was finally standing up for myself. There was a moment of dead silence on the phone. He put me on hold, and after a period of time, came back on line and told me he would pay me what I was asking so I accepted the position. I took another big cut in salary but knew that I just needed to get out from my current situation in order to maintain my sanity. I later learned that the new administration wanted me gone and believed that by having me go to a long-term care facility, I would be forgotten and was never to be heard from again; they were mistaken.

Before I left my director position, I had been working on a project with the manager of risk management, and she was scheduled to give a presentation to the Board of Trustees of the corporation and asked me to attend with her even though I had already started my new job. The director of nurses was present and was asked a basic question by one of the board members that she should have been able to answer but she was unable to do so. Knowing the answer and watching her fidget I wondered whether I should help her by answering the question or just let her stew. For nursing's sake, my decision was to answer the question and save her neck. She never thanked me for that, but a year later, when she was having trouble with her managers, she asked me to come to meet with her as she tried to pick my brain as to what she could do. I wondered why she had called me as before she did not seem to value my opinion. I told her I was too busy to help her and left her office. About a year later, when it was finally discovered that she did not know as much as she professed, she was asked to leave.

The sub-acute unit was classified as a long-term care facility and would be caring for comatose patients on ventilators. Some of my friends questioned me as to why I would leave my position over critical care, telemetry, emergency, short stay, PACU, endoscopy, and operating room to move to a subacute unit. They thought I had lost my mind, but I knew in my heart that a change needed to be made. Because the subacute unit was considered a long-term care facility, one of the positions required was a director of staff development. Consequently, a director of staff development from one of the organization's long-term care facilities was brought onboard to work with me. Pam S. was her name, and we eventually became very good friends. Before she came onboard, she came to me and told me that she really did not know anything about ventilators, and my response to her was that it was okay because I did not know anything about long-term care, so we would teach each other, and together we should make a good team. We ended up making a great team!

The management company sent me to one of their subacute units in Glendale to orient to subacute care with the clinical director of the unit. He took one look took at me and stated, "Well, we will see whether you can keep up with me."

Oh please, I thought. *Keep up with you? I can probably work circles around you.* This turned out to be true as he was a smoker and was on a break every thirty minutes. I oriented one weekend with him and then came back to our unit to begin to admit patients. The management company had a nurse who would visit hospitals to identify patients needing subacute care and referred them to our unit. We soon were busy caring for our patients. We eventually admitted thirty-three patients who could not move themselves and had to be turned every two hours in order to prevent skin breakdown. One of our patients had ALS (Lou Gehrig's disease) and was paralyzed from the neck down. He was very alert but had to communicate via a computer as he had a tracheostomy, and he was very demanding. However, he was our patient, and we took care of him the best way we could.

During the entire five years that we headed up this unit, not one patient developed a decubitus ulcer, and our unit gained a reputation of being an excellent care facility which led to us having a waiting list of families wanting to transfer their loved ones to our unit. We had one patient who developed a red spot on his hip one day, and I was quite upset. When I called the certified nursing assistant (CNA) to my office to ask her why her patient had developed a red spot, her response to me was that she just did not have time to turn him. My response to her was that her job was to turn the patients every two hours so they would not develop a red spot, and my job as the director was to turn in a time card for her so that she would get paid every two weeks. So I asked her if I did not have time to turn in a time card for her would it be okay that she did not receive a paycheck. I told her that we both had a job to do in order to make sure the patients were taken care of on our unit.

She told me it would never happen again, and I said, "I am sure that it won't." I never had another problem with any patient getting a red spot as the CNAs knew and understood the importance of turning patients and the problems that could occur if they did not do their job.

As the director of nursing, I was told that I had the ultimate say as to whether we could accept a new patient that was being presented to us. I had to decide whether we had the capability to care for the patient. There were a couple of times when I had to deny the admission of a patient as I did not feel that we could meet the patient's needs. One day, I received a call from the nursing director of the management company telling me that the owner of the company felt that I was refusing too many patients. After explaining my reasons and using a few choice words, I was never asked about my reasons for refusing a patient again. We had excellent outcomes, and they were making money.

After a year of success in running this unit, the management of the company would send new nursing directors to orient with me on our unit. We had a management agreement with the company who had started the program, and for the first two years of the contract, the hospital did not make any money on this service as all of the profits were going to the management company. Once we were finished with the two-year contract, I asked the administrator not to renew the contract. He was concerned as the contract included a nurse who was able to recruit patients for the unit. I told him that we no longer needed that recruiter as we had a waiting list of patients whose families were waiting for an opening so they could transfer their loved one to our unit. He finally agreed not to renew the contract, and the unit soon began making money. We maintained a full census and a waiting list of patients and passed our first Joint Commission survey with flying colors. When I talked with the finance accountant about the financial status of the unit, he informed me that after a year without the contract, the unit was paying for all its direct and indirect costs and contributing over three quarters of a million dollars to the organization. Our unit experienced several success stories, and its success was featured in several articles in medical journals.

Our subacute program had a policy that allowed pet therapy, and so we allowed patient's cats, dogs, rabbits, and other pets to visit the individual patients. We noted that pet therapy made a difference in the response of our patients. One of our patients who was semi-comatose loved horses and had her own special horse. When the staff told me that they wanted to be able to have her husband bring her horse to our facility, I put my foot down and told them that we would not be having a horse come down the hallway to see the patient. However, I told them that we could allow her husband to bring the horse to the back of the facility where we had a piece of grass and take the patient out to the horse. So we placed the patient on a gurney and took her outside to see her horse. The horse immediately recognized his owner, and the patient knew her horse. After that visit with her horse, a change came over the patient, and two weeks later, she awakened from her semi-comatose state, and eventually, she was able to be discharged from the facility. All in all, because of the special programs we had, seventeen of our semi-comatose patients awakened from their comas, and our unit was a star in the organization. Along with pet therapy, we employed different methods of stimulation on our patients, such as having the families record their dinner conversations at home and then bring the recordings in, and we would place earpieces in their loved ones' ears and allowed them to listen to the family speaking as hearing is the last one of our senses that remains. It was amazing the response we received from those type of actions.

CHAPTER 17

Obtaining a Degree

When I finally decided that I could go back to school to obtain my bachelor's degree, I went to meet with the nursing department at the local state college. After inquiring about what steps I needed to take in order to obtain my Bachelor of Science in nursing (BSN) degree, I was informed that because I was a diploma graduate, I basically had to go back to school and start all over. They would not give me credit for any of my courses that I had already taken. I was depressed to receive such news, and it did not seem fair to me, so I looked for other options. Luckily for me, I was friends with the dean of the School of Health Sciences, Dr. Carolyn D., at Fresno City College, a local community college. She was also serving as the coordinator of an RN to BSN program through a Statewide Nursing Consortium located at California State University, Dominguez Hills in Southern California. She informed me that if I registered for twelve units at Fresno City College, I would be given credit for thirty units from my nursing school program that could be transferred. This was music to my ears to have this other option, so in 1985, I registered for the first of the twelve units at the community college. History, chemistry, and sociology were the courses taken. I completed the twelve units and then transferred to the RN to BSN program. In 1988, I took my first class from Fresno City College, an ethics class offered at the local high school, and found myself sitting in class with some of my older son's classmates who had just graduated from high school. I was a little embarrassed sitting in class with them, but soon realized that my life experiences could be an asset to the class, which allowed me to enjoy it. I was on my way to receiving my degree and was able to use tuition reimbursement at my work to help pay for my educational expenses. Due to working full-tine, I could only go to school on a part-time basis, so it took me until 1996 to complete my BSN degree. This program required travel to different parts of the San Joaquin Valley in order to take the classes needed, and I shared rides with three other nurses who worked at St. Agnes Hospital, which made traveling to the various location where the classes were offered less of a chore. I enjoyed all of the classes except for my statistics class. Statistics was a real challenge as it involved math, and math was never fun for me. Buddy study sessions with my friend Kim allowed me to better understand, and ultimately, pass the course. With my background being critical care, I was able to contribute greatly in our physical assessment course. After many years of hard work, all the units required to obtain my Bachelor of Science in Nursing degree (BSN) were completed, and I felt a great load taken off of my shoulders. I no longer had to be embarrassed to be serving in a management position without having a degree. My happiness was expressed in tears of joy throughout the entire graduation ceremony.

In 1991, my mother, who was only sixty-seven years old, began complaining of abdominal pain, and after much encouragement, she made an appointment to see her doctor. I called her that evening to get the results of her visit. She informed me that he had ordered some medication for her and because she could not pronounce the name of the medicine, she spelled it out for me. When she spelled out the word *Librax*, I could not believe that he had just ordered a tranquilizer for her and sent her home; no lab work or x-rays. I told her to call him back and ask him for an upper and lower gastrointestinal series as well as a gallbladder test. Her doctor did order the tests and found that she had pancreatic cancer and told her she had six months to live. When I called and spoke with the doctor, he informed me that she really only had about three months to live.

My mother refused to take any type of cancer therapy; she did try some supplements, but eventually gave up on those and began to plan for her funeral. My brothers and sisters and I all agreed that we would take care of her at home and took turns caring for her. My sister Esther who was a teacher and was off for the summer would come on Monday evening and stay until Thursday when she would return back home. My other sister and I would then take over her care. She became weaker and weaker and could no longer eat and eventually died in July of that year. Losing our mother was very hard on all of us, and we comforted each other as best we could.

The following year, my seventeen-year-old nephew Jason and his brother Justin were involved in a traffic accident, and unfortunately, Jason lost his life. We were all in a state of shock when we were notified that Labor Day weekend in 1992. We all travelled to Prunedale to support our sister and brother-in-law, as well as our niece and nephew. Jason's life was taken way too soon and his death impacted all of us deeply. Our nephew Justin had a long recovery period with additional surgery to repair muscles in his arm and heal the burn scars.

Prior to my mother being diagnosed with cancer, my father had been diagnosed with prostate cancer. His was slow growing, and he was given radiation treatments. In early 1993, my father's cancer had metastasized, and he was getting worse; he was having much more pain and he was placed in hospice care. Because we were all working, we hired his half-sister who had worked previously as a CNA to take care of him during the day. The six of us took turns paying her salary, and my younger sister moved in with him to be there at night. We were able to start him on a morphine pump to help control his pain. We, again, were able to care for him at home and allowed him to die at home just like our mother. He died in September 1993. We held a rosary service and Mass for him just as we had done for our mother. However, he had requested to be cremated, and we respected his wishes so we had a service for him with just immediate family at the cemetery when we entombed his ashes alongside our mother. We all felt like orphans now that both our parents were gone, and we held on to our husbands/wives and our children. Having had three deaths three years in a row, we all held our breaths during 1994 and breathed a big sigh of relief when we made it through the year without a death in our family. Before my mother died, she had asked me to do my best to keep the six brothers and sisters together after she and our father were gone, and so a promise was made. Our mother was happiest when she had us all together by her side. So I went to my brother and told him about the promise made and asked him to either help me or get the hell out of my way. Luckily, he agreed to help me, and we have kept a close bond between the six of us, getting together for as many holidays as we can. If one of us is in trouble, the rest are right there by their side to be of support. We know that when we are able to be together, our parents are up in heaven smiling,

Even through our losses, our lives continued. After receiving my BSN degree, I thought about stopping my education but decided instead to work toward my master's degree (MSN). Being in a school mode, I decided it made sense to continue. My three friends who had also received their BSN degree stated that they too would go on to get their masters. However, one of the three learned that she was pregnant, and because she was a Type I diabetic, she decided that she could not continue. The other two started the MSN program but quit after one semester. I considered quitting myself especially on Saturday mornings when having to get up to go to school. I would ask my husband to tell me again why it was necessary for me to get up from my warm and comfortable bed, and he would always tell me that it would pay off in the future. So it was off to class.

I selected the educator role for my master's degree, and my classes were held all over the state. Every other weekend required me to travel to a city where the class was being offered. I would drive down to Bakersfield on Friday night after getting off work, stay with my cousin Emily, and get up early the next morning to drive to Pomona or Escondido where my class was being held. I would return home on Sunday evening and then go back to work on Monday morning. In between, there was always a paper to write. My home office floor was a disaster with references and articles that I was using to write my papers, scattered all over the floor. Other classes required me to drive to Stockton, find a hotel to stay the night, and go to class on Saturday afternoon and all day Sunday. I would return home on Sunday evening, and then it was back to work on Monday morning. Somedays, when looking back, my mind questions how this was accomplished considering that my life was also filled with extracurricular activities like attending professional meetings. It was a good thing that my sons were grown. My computer and I became very good friends and a huge amount of paper and ink were used.

CHAPTER 18

Losing a Soul Mate

1997 was both a good and bad year. I was nominated a third time for the RN of the Year award, and the third time was the charm as I won the award. Having been nominated two times before and not being selected, I was not expecting to win again this year. I had flown to Orlando to present at the National Subacute Conference and was flying back into Fresno the night of the event. Since we were delayed in leaving Atlanta, I missed my flight in Phoenix and had to wait for the next flight. The award dinner started at 6:00 p.m., so I called my husband and asked him to bring my change of clothes to the airport so I could change in the airport bathroom. We barely made it to the event on time. Not expecting to win, I did not hear my name called when my name was announced as this year's winner. It was a wonderful surprise and was so happy that both my son and my husband had been in attendance to witness my award presentation. That was the last event ever attended with my husband.

In June of this same year, my husband of twenty-seven years and my soul mate—who was a diabetic and had been disabled for two years due to losing part of his right foot—now was faced with having to endure an amputation of part of his left foot. He had been a patient in Community Hospital a year earlier for four days, and none of the nursing staff bothered to check his left foot to make sure there was no pressure from the slipper sock that was put on his foot to keep it warm. Since we were in the middle of a Joint Commission survey, I did not bother to check his left foot, thinking that this was being done by the nursing staff. After all, he had already lost part of his right foot, so good nursing care would dictate that the nurse would check his left foot to make sure that the skin was intact and that there was no pressure on the foot. When I helped him get dressed to take him home and took off the slipper sock, there was a huge indentation from the seam on the slipper sock that had pressed on the bottom of his left big toe and caused the indentation. Prior to this, there was nothing wrong with his left foot. Seeing the huge indentation caused me to gasp as I knew the problem this could cause. Sure enough, the indentation turned into an ulceration. For one year, we tried different techniques to try to save his toes but to no avail. It was very hard to understand why the nurses caring for him who knew that he was in the hospital for an amputation revision on his right foot would not check his good left foot to make sure that no problem was developing. The fact that this was the hospital of my employment led me to restrain my anger that this had happened.

When my husband realized what he was in for, he decided to write a letter to the hospital complaining about his care. The hospital risk manager responded and stated that the hospital was not at fault for what had happened. Rather than take responsibility for not preventing the incident, they took no responsibility. This angered my husband, and he decided to get an attorney and sue the hospital. No lawyer in the city would take the case. He had to go out of town to find an attorney. Because of my administrative position at the facility, I shared with him that my role would not allow me to be involved in this suit and he would have to handle it on his own; I did not even want to know the name of his attorney. He finally found an attorney in Walnut Creek who agreed to take his case. He met with his attorney and discussed his case and began the process of suing the hospital, the maker of the slipper sock, and one of his doctors.

Because his left big toe had not healed for over a year, his surgeon scheduled him for surgery, and on June 4, he went into surgery for an amputation of his toes on his left foot. My husband did not believe in advanced directives, and therefore had not filled out this form, so two nights before his surgery I asked him what he wanted me to do if something bad happened to him during surgery. He asked, "Like what?"

I said, "Like if in case your heart should stop or you have a stroke."

Since he had already been disabled for two years, he informed me that he did not want to be kept alive on machines. I understood his wishes and cried myself to sleep that night. To this day, I don't know if this was a premonition or I just wanted to make sure that his wishes were clearly known but was happy that the question had been asked.

On the early morning of June 4, 1997, we went to the hospital where he was admitted for surgery. He was prepped for the procedure, and as we waited for the surgery staff to pick him up and take him to the surgical suite, I kissed him on the lips and felt no response from him, so I kissed him again and still no response. Kissing him the third time with still no response, I thought it was probably due to the medications he had been given. The surgery staff came to pick him up, and I went to my office. About 12:00 p.m., his doctor called me and told me that the surgery had gone well, and he was now in the recovery room. He informed me that he had been able to save most of his left foot, and I was happy to hear that piece of news and knew Joe would be happy. My calendar showed an appointment for 12:30, so I decided to wait until after my appointment before seeing him. My appointment was completed a little after 1:00 p.m., and when opening the door to the administrative offices, the hospital chaplain was running down the hall. She told me that she had been looking for me as Joe had coded in the recovery room.

We both ran up the stairs to the second floor and rushed into the recovery room where my husband was being attended to in the back of the room. I started moving toward that direction but was stopped by one of the staff and taken into a side room. A little while later, one of the staff escorted me into a room just outside the recovery room where I was instructed to wait. My boss and another vice president were standing just outside the recovery room and the look on their faces told me how bad they felt. A little while later, one of the recovery room nurses came into the room and told me that my husband's heart rate had slowed significantly and he was being given medication.

No problem, I thought. *A little atropine will help his heart beat faster.*

About ten minutes later, another recovery room nurse came in and informed me that his heart head gone into an agonal rhythm. Having taught cardiac classes for the critical care and telemetry nurses, my knowledge of cardiac rhythms came to mind, and I instantly knew that this was not good and that I was going to be a widow at the age of fifty. My friend, the hospital cardiologist, was called to the code and then he came to talk to me. He told me he wanted to take him to the cardiac catheterization lab and look at his heart. He and the cardiology staff tried desperately to save his life, but it was futile. He had suffered a major heart attack due to a blockage of the main coronary artery. I was told that I should call my sons who were both living in San Diego at the time and tell them about what had happened. I had already called my sister who lived in town, and she was at my side. Having to call my sons and tell them about their father was one of the hardest phone calls I have ever had to make. They left San Diego for Fresno right away.

My husband was taken to the intensive care unit on life support, and walking down that corridor to the ICU—a hall that I had walked many times before—was very difficult. The cardiac surgeon, my friend, was called to place him on a cardiac assist device. The critical care physician asked me how long before our sons would arrive, and when informed that they would not be arriving until about 10:00 p.m., he stated that he was not sure we had that much time. I told him that we must keep him alive until our sons arrived. I also insisted that an electroencephalogram (EEG) be done and read that night so we could determine how much brain activity there was as I remembered what he had told me about not wanting to be kept alive on machines. My sons arrived around 10:30 p.m., and the rest of my family and close friends were called by my sister Mattie and they all came to give me support. He was placed on numerous medications to help keep his blood pressure at normal levels for perfusion but to no avail. His EEG indicated very little brain activity.

The next day, my sons and I discussed his wishes, and we made the decision to disconnect him from life support. This was the hardest decision I have ever had to make; my head told me one thing and my heart told me something else, but in the end when it was determined that there was no hope for survival, we had to respect his wishes and let him go home to God. After saying our good-byes, his ventilator was turned off, and my sons and I stood at his bedside as he took a few last breaths and his heart stopped beating. He was gone. My soulmate and their father was gone.

After making this difficult decision, I desperately needed the nurses who were my employees and friends to tell me that I had made the right decision to let him go, but they were not able to do so. I was beginning to feel guilty until my friend, a social worker, John, came up to me before we left the hospital and told me, "Pilar, you did the right thing."

Whew, I was then able to take that guilt off of my back and went home to begin to make plans for his funeral. Making plans for his funeral service was very difficult and tiring; thank goodness for my family who was by my side every step of the way. Trying to choose a casket was hard, but I had always said that Joe was the "wind beneath my wings," so when a casket that had those exact words on the inside of the lid was viewed, I said, "That is the one." The cost was not important to me, and I did not even ask about the price as it did not matter; we had found the right casket for him.

Many people attended his funeral, both family and friends. Many of my coworkers attended and sent flowers. In fact, my home looked like a florist shop with so many different types of flowers and plants sent by friends. We had a catered reception at our house after the burial service, and it was comforting to be surrounded by everyone. One of my friends who was a lawyer gave me a piece of advice that he gives to other people. He said, "Pilar, don't make any major changes or decisions for one year; don't buy any big item or sell anything for a year."

When most of the people left, I was exhausted and took a short nap. My son Steve was the last one to leave a couple of days later, and before he left, he said to me, "Mom, please don't cry," so I kept it together until after he left and then I went inside my house, grabbed my husband's picture, drew it close to my heart and fell down on the floor and began to cry. My crying did not last long, however, as a nurse friend came by to visit me and share her condolences.

One week after his death, the position of vice president of continuing care was offered to me by my boss; this was the position I was interviewing for when my husband had his event. I accepted the position then left town to spend a few days with a friend at the coast. I remember being called into a special meeting before I was scheduled to return to work. I drove to the meeting, parked my car, and before I crossed the street to enter the hospital, I suddenly stopped in my tracks. Feeling frozen as I stood there on the corner, my mind was racing, and I wondered whether I could actually walk back into the hospital where my husband had just died. I decided that I was either going to walk across the street and go to the meeting or I was going to turn around and leave and never go back into that hospital again. I decided to walk across the street and go to the meeting.

Since I had started the master's in nursing program, I called my instructor and informed her of my husband's death. She was very understanding and told me that I could drop out for one semester and still remain in the program. Knowing myself I knew that dropping out for even just one semester would be a mistake as there was a good chance I would not return to finish the program. Realizing that I would not be dropping out for the semester, she was able to find a one-unit course, gerontology, that I could take that next semester and that was enough to help me remain and finish the program on time.

CHAPTER 19
Living as a Single

Having never lived by myself before, I was now facing that test. Going from living at home with my parents and family to living in the dorm at nursing school to sharing an apartment with a friend, then back home until I got married had not prepared me for living alone. I was scared and wondered how I could go on living without him. I took a month off from work to take care of all of the paperwork and notifications that had to be taken care of after his death. I tried speaking to a grief counselor but did not feel that he was able to help me deal with my grief. Instead, I decided to write a journal to express my feelings, making notations daily—sometimes with my tears dripping down on the pages. On Sunday mornings after church, I would go to the store and buy flowers and visit his grave; this was my routine. As time passed, I found myself writing less and not visiting the cemetery as often. Returning to work kept my mind off the loss during the day, but upon returning home in the evening, I would immediately turn on the television to hear some sort of sound in the house.

Life was not easy for me. I was okay during the week as I was around people. The weekends, on the other hand, were very hard as I was all by myself. Two of my husband's sisters had basically abandoned me and were not very nice; his baby sister and her husband did stay in contact and visited me, along with his brother and his wife. I found myself going to the malls and shopping for unneeded items just to be around people on weekends; I became a shopaholic but was able to curb my behavior after realizing the impact of my actions.

The attorney that my husband had contacted on his own was in the midst of gathering information from my husband to build the case when my husband died. While gathering all of my husband's possessions, I found his attorney's business card in his wallet. Thinking that he needed to be notified of my husband's death, I called him and informed him that my husband had died. My thought was that he would just close the case, but instead, he informed me that now the case had become a wrongful death suit and everyone would be involved. Informing him of my position at the hospital, he decided that he wanted to meet with my sons and discuss their father's case with them. My sons made arrangements to come home so that they could meet with him. They both decided that since their father had started this case, they wanted to see it through for him. Their words to me were, "You may get married again and have another husband, but we will never have another dad." Since they were both over the age of eighteen, they were adults and able to make their own decision. The case proceeded.

Eventually, the case ended in a settlement, but the fact that the hospital was one of the defendants caused me discomfort as I was questioned by my boss about the suit on the request of the hospital attorney and accused by others of suing the hospital. It was very stressful for me as I felt people were viewing me as some kind of a traitor. Besides stress, my feelings were of embarrassment that this had happened at my hospital as I had always been proud of the care that was given to patients, but this was just poor nursing care. I informed my boss of my noninvolvement in the suit and that it was my sons who had decided to move forward, and because they were both adults, I could not tell them what to do; it was their decision. When finally leaving my employment with the hospital, I felt a real sense of relief from all of the pressure. I was now free and knew that I would never have to walk into that hospital again.

Prior to my husband's death, I had committed to do a presentation in Boise, Idaho, in July, and we had made plans to use this trip as a vacation, choosing to travel to Yellowstone National Park as a side trip. My very good friends, Ana and Carlos decided that they would make plans to go with me to Idaho and Yellowstone as they had not yet made vacation plans. I was in pain and depressed and suicide crossed my mind during that trip more than once but could not do that to my sons and family. I wondered why the sun still came up each morning and then realized that the world and life does not stop for anyone regardless of the situation. There was a choice to make, I could either become an alcoholic to try to drown my sorrows or pull myself up by the bootstraps and get on with life. I chose the latter.

Listening to advice of my friend who was a lawyer, no big decisions or changes were made in my life for one year other than taking on this new position. After the year, I decided to give up my job and move to San Diego where both of my sons, my sister, and brother were living. I put my house on the market and began looking for a home in the San Diego area. My parents had died so there was really no one in the area except one sister to keep me here. I gave up my position and agreed to stay on to orient the two new vice presidents who had been hired. I was having trouble selling my house, and my plans for moving just were not moving well. My CEO and other leaders did not want me to leave, and so my CEO made me an offer I just could not refuse by offering me the position of vice president of the education department. I agreed to stay and take on this new role.

In this position, I was asked to meet with a community leader and a principal of a local elementary school. They were concerned about the unemployment rate of the parents of the children in the school, and since the hospital was the largest employer in the area, they asked to meet with us to see if there was a program that could be developed. My boss asked me to develop the program, and since it was almost Christmas, we agreed to meet again after the New Year holiday.

My sons and I realized that we could not spend Christmas at home without my husband and their father; it would not be the same, and we needed to do something different. So I booked a cruise for the three of us over the Christmas holiday and went on a Mexican Riviera cruise to Puerto Vallarta, Mazatlán, and Cabo San Lucas.

On Christmas day, my sons and I were sitting in a bar in Mazatlán having a drink, and my son said to me, "If anyone had ever told me that I would be sitting in a bar with my mother on Christmas Day, I would have told them they were crazy." And yet there we were, at Señor Frog's having a drink on Christmas Day.

The second Christmas after his death, we still were not ready to spend the holiday at home, so I reserved a condo in Maui, and we spent the holiday on the island. We had a wonderful time, enjoyed our time together, and were able to get through the holiday without him. By the third year, we were able to go back to spending the holiday at home. We had made it through the holidays without Joe for a second year, and we were healing.

The night before my boss and I were supposed to meet with the community leader and principal, I realized that nothing had been put together for our upcoming meeting as I had been asked. Sitting down at my computer and putting my brain to work, I developed a program called the Jefferson Job Institute. It was a six-month program that would include both classroom instruction as well as volunteer work in different areas of the hospital. Working with Fresno Unified, the county of Fresno's GAIN program (welfare), and the hospital, we were able to have classroom instruction for three months for the participants and then three months of actual hands-on volunteer work in the hospital. At the end of the six months, if the students had been successful, dependable, and demonstrated initiative, and if there was an open position, they could be offered employment. The program proved to be very successful with participants gaining employment with the hospital;

some who are still working there today. Participants were able to buy their first car or home, and the GAIN department said that this was the best program they had for getting people off of the welfare rolls. Eventually, up to four schools became a part of the program, and family members of successful participants could not wait to be a part of the program as well. In addition, another plus was that the children of the participants who were students in the four schools would see their parents studying, which would encourage then to study as well.

CHAPTER 20

Moving On with Life

In 1999, I was selected as one of the Top Ten Business and Professional Women in Fresno County and was recognized at a luncheon along with nine other women. I was nominated for all the work I had done in the community and at work. My family was in attendance and helped to share in my happiness. Having worked with students and mentoring thirty-five of them, I was also recognized by the California Wellness Foundation and given an award of $25,000 to use as I pleased, along with a medal. The organization had selected three individuals from throughout the state to recognize for their work with helping minority students and presented them with the award. I was invited to Los Angeles to receive my award with the other two individuals selected in California for this honor. This was a great honor for me, and I was very happy to have been selected a winner.

This same year, we were having a severe shortage of nurses, and we were desperate to employ more nurses. I was at a Community Hospital board retreat at Tenaya Lodge in Yosemite with my friend Dr. Carol D., who was a member of the hospital's Board of Trustees. At the end of the day, we were sitting on the patio having a glass of wine, and I shared with her how desperate we were to get more nurses and we needed Fresno City College to graduate more of them. She told me she only had forty-six slots, and they were on the lottery system for selecting students to enter their program. I told her that we needed to do something to change that because the hospital had sixteen employees who had completed all of their prerequisites courses for the nursing program and were just waiting to be selected by their lottery system before they could start. We decided to have another glass of wine to brainstorm what we could do. At the end of our second glass of wine, we had drawn out a plan on a napkin called the Nursing Paradigm Program, a contract education program where the hospital would pay the college money to add another class of nursing students and would provide clinical instructors to help the students in their clinical rotation. We figured out it would cost the hospital about $80,000 for this program. Considering that it usually cost a hospital about $50,000 to recruit one nurse, we believed that the $80,000 for sixteen nurses was a good investment, and since I had signing authority for up to $100,000, we moved ahead.

After the announcement was made, I ran into one of the hospital board members who asked me if this should have not come before the board for approval. Because I am a believer in asking for forgiveness rather than permission, depending on the situation I just asked, "Oh, was I supposed to do that?" To Dr. Carol D and me, this was a no-brainer.

Since the nurses would graduate in 2000, we named it Paradigm 2000. It was not long before the other hospitals in the area heard about this program and called me. They wanted in, so we developed a committee with members from five different hospitals. We began this eighteen-month program, and each hospital was allowed five spaces for their staff. If a hospital did not need all five slots, they could give the extra slots to the other hospitals so we could fill the twenty-five positions. The students who were hospital employees and had been waiting for their name to be called from the lottery were thrilled, and the hospitals were happy to be gaining additional nurses. Since these new graduates were already employees of the hospitals, they did not require orientation to the hospital. They committed to working for the hospital for two years after completing the Paradigm Program, and it became more popular than the regular twenty-four-month nursing program.

To be eligible for the Paradigm Program, the students had to have completed all of their prerequisites, be an employee of the hospital in any department, and be recommended by their manager or supervisor. Over the ten-year period that the program ran, we graduated an additional 750 nurses for the Central Valley, which really helped to solve the nursing shortage in the area. Many of the graduates of this program have come up to us at meetings and thanked us for implementing this special program which allowed them to become a registered nurse.

I was at a nurse leadership conference in San Diego when a nurse came up to me and said, "You probably do not remember me, but I went through the Paradigm Program and became a nurse because of your efforts to expand the program at Fresno City College. My name had been in the lotto for two years but had never been called. Through the Paradigm Program, I was able to graduate, I went back and got my bachelor's and master's degrees, and I am now working on my doctorate!" Her comments were very much appreciated.

After two years of grieving my husband's loss and tired of living alone, I decided it was time to meet someone for companionship. I had been asked by a couple of men at the hospital if I was ready to start dating again but did not want to date anyone at the hospital so as not to feed the rumor mill. I just told them not yet. I felt bad lying to them, but felt it was for the best. I decided to take this opportunity to meet someone new, and at the time, the local paper carried a personal section that ran every Friday, so I began looking at the personals. There were several interesting notices, and listening to their taped messages before beginning to respond to any of them gave me a head start. The very first one sounded very sincere, so I decided to leave a response message. Making contact with others and meeting them for lunch in public places worked well. While they were all nice, I was not interested in pursuing the relationship further after our first meeting. I did not plan to marry again but just wanted some companionship. After about two months, I met my future husband.

My phone rang early on a Monday morning, and I thought it was probably my son who usually called me on Sunday night but had not done so that Sunday; I therefore assumed it was him calling. When hearing a voice that I did not recognize, his first words were an apology for calling so early in the morning but told me that he had been trying to reach me and had been unsuccessful. Because I was going to school, working on my master's, and traveling out of town every other weekend to attend my classes, it took us a long time to meet. We had been talking on the phone for two months before we actually met for lunch and a movie. By the time of our first date, my feeling was that I knew him after talking to him on the phone every day for two months. On our second date, he invited me to breakfast at Bass Lake, and after breakfast, we sat by the lake and just talked. After three years of dating, we decided to marry. We both loved Mariachi music and had purchased a table for the yearly Mariachi festival inviting his father, sisters, my brother and sister, and their spouses to join us. He had found a florist at the event, bought a rose for each of the women in attendance at our table and had them delivered but none for me. He then came back to the table with a dozen red roses for me and proposed and I said yes.

Completion of my master's program in 2001 was a great relief and then I submitted my project for approval. I had never done this before and did not ask anyone to read it for me before submitting it. That was a mistake. I was called by the coordinator and told that my project had not been accepted as it had not passed. She asked me if I had asked anyone to read it before submitting it and my response was "No." She strongly encouraged me to do so with my next submission. She told me that I would have one more chance to submit my project again and that if it did not pass a second time, then the entire master's program would have to be repeated. I was upset and embarrassed at not having passed and vowed to do so the second time. My staff at work gave me a party in celebration, and I did not have the heart to tell them about my status. In fact, no one was told of my situation until later. I redid my project, and this time, had two professors read it for me and they told me it would pass. I waited anxiously to hear back from the school as to the status of my project and was very happy when I received the phone call telling me of my successful submission and passing the program. *Yeah!* MSN could now be added after my name.

Having completed my master's program, it was now time to concentrate on planning my wedding. Because my fiancé had been married before and divorced, we had to work with the Catholic Church in order to get an annulment of his first wedding before we would be allowed to marry in the church. My friend, Father Donal, who was the Catholic priest assigned to the hospital helped us with the paperwork and follow-up. We set a date of April 20, 2002 for our marriage at the Catholic church in Sanger but also had a back-up plan with a minister to be married at the Belmont Country Club where we were having our reception, in case the annulment did not come through in time. We sent out invitations and continued to work on our wedding plans.

One day, Father Donal came into my office and asked me, "How do you feel about St. Therese Church?"

At which time, I asked him, "Are you telling me we are not getting married at St. Mary's Church in Sanger?" and he said yes.

Apparently, Father Donal had received word that the annulment had been approved but because the priests in Sanger had not yet received the paperwork, they would not let us get married in their church in Sanger. Father Donal had talked with the Monsignor at St. Therese, and he had agreed to let us get married at his church. So we had to send out new invitations informing our guests that we were getting married on April 20 but that the venue had changed. So we had a beautiful marriage at St. Therese Church and then went to our reception at the Belmont Country Club where we and our 180 guests all had a good time. The next morning, we flew to Cancun for our honeymoon.

I had served in the role of vice president of education for a year when the new HR director convinced the corporate CEO that there were too many vice presidents in the organization. Consequently, in 2002, seven vice president positions were downgraded to director positions; the pay remained the same, but our titles were changed. The interesting thing about this move was that the seven positions that were downgraded were all women. The Board of Trustees was concerned that we would file a lawsuit claiming discrimination, and I suppose we could have but none of us resorted to that action. People would come up to me and ask me if I was all right; my response to them was that I had just survived the loss of my husband and that this was peanuts compared to that. I did consider leaving the organization and even asked my boss to just lay me off, but he did not want to do that. When the corporate CEO found out that I was thinking of leaving, he called me to his office and asked me what it would take to keep me from leaving. My request was that I be given a letter in writing stating that if I were ever to be laid-off, that it would be at the vice president level and not at the director level, as there was a six-month difference in terms of the severance pay. He asked me if I did not trust them, and my immediate response was "No." By that afternoon, my letter signed by the corporate CEO was handed to me, stating that if I were ever to be laid off, it would be at the vice president level which carried with it a year's severance package versus six months. I took the letter and put it in my safety deposit box for safekeeping. My work as executive director of education continued, and we implemented new programs which benefited the staff.

In 2003, the idea of developing a recognition program for nurses who had given a lifetime of work and dedication to the profession came to mind. Being a sports fan, I knew that sports had a mechanism to recognize great players. I figured that if baseball and football could have a hall of fame for their players, why not one for nurses to recognize the achievements of great valley nurses in different areas of nursing. We convened the presidents of the Nursing Leadership Council, Sigma Theta Tau, Mu Nu Chapter, and Fresno State School of Nursing, and we would meet every two weeks at Uncle Harry's Bagel Shop where we would brainstorm and eventually develop and introduce the San Joaquin Valley Nursing Hall of Fame. I personally gave a $500 donation to Fresno State via a special nursing fund to get it started. We developed and introduced the nomination criteria, evaluation scoring sheet, the special medallion and the plaque that would hold the names of the inductees. The fruits of our labor came to fruition when we had our first celebration and induction ceremony in 2004 inducting two nurse leaders. I was inducted into the Hall of Fame in 2005. Each year, we have this event where nurses are recognized for lifetime achievements and their name is placed on a plaque in the hallway of the School of Nursing at Fresno State. A special medallion is given to each person who is inducted into the Hall of Fame. So each year, dedicated and deserving nurses are nominated and inducted into the Nursing Hall of Fame.

CHAPTER 21

Chief Nurse Executive

I am a firm believer that everything happens for a reason. Shortly after the change in title took place, the opportunity to be the chief nurse at the newly built Fresno Heart Hospital came before me. My goal from the beginning was to eventually become the chief nurse at a hospital, and now, I was being given that opportunity. The Fresno Heart Hospital was jointly owned by a group of cardiologists and Community Regional Medical Center, the doctors having a 49 percent interest and the community hospital with a 51 percent interest. A CEO and CFO had already been hired, along with the Director of Human Resources (HR), but they needed to hire a nursing director. I accepted the position after negotiating my starting salary and began the hard work of getting the hospital ready to open. The hospital was beautiful and looked more like a hotel than a hospital. The special tile on the outside of the hospital had cost a fortune and the furnishings throughout were elegant.

My initial job was to hire the nursing staff and get the hospital ready for inspection by the state so that we could open. This meant establishing all of the policies and procedures, setting up the units with supplies, approving purchases of equipment needed, and training of staff on the electronic medical record that we would be using and identifying the leadership for the staff. My previous management experience had prepared me well for this job, but the job was made difficult because of the CEO who did not really understand operations. He was more interested on making the facility look like a fancy hotel rather than being realistic about how the hospital needed to function. As an example, he felt that the crash carts distracted from the beauty of the unit and wanted them to be hidden and stored in cabinets rather than to be left sitting by the side of the nurse's station where it could be readily available for use. He did not like the bedspreads that had been ordered as they were not pretty enough. He wanted fancy bedspreads on the patient beds. When informed that this would be an infection control problem as the bedspreads would need to be washed between patients, he was not happy. He insisted that the nurses could fold up the bedspreads and put them in the closet before the admission of the patient to the bed. To me this seemed like it defeated the purpose of having beautiful bedspreads on the beds. In addition, the nurses were not going to have time to fold the bedspreads before admitting the patients to the beds. He wanted the lab and pharmacy to report to him rather than the director of patient care services or chief nurse.

He refused to listen to the directions of the corporate CEO as he wanted to do things his way. He would not listen to individuals who had more operational experience than him. As an example, he insisted on having the state come and inspect the hospital for opening before we had everything in place, including medications and supplies. When the state is called to come and inspect a hospital for opening, they expect everything to be in place and that you are ready to open the hospital the next day. We were not anywhere near that point, and even though I told him so, he insisted on proceeding. He informed me that I was upsetting a couple of the people who reported to him due to my telling them that there were certain requirements that needed to be changed in order to meet code. They did not want to believe me, but in the end, they had to make the changes which I had told them needed to be made. I finally told the CEO if he had wanted a wall flower as the chief nurse then he had chosen the wrong person for this position as I was not a wall flower, and my job was to tell him what operationally needed to be done in order to make us successful. The state inspectors came as scheduled, and when they realized at 10:30 a.m. that we were not ready for the inspection, they decided to leave; we had wasted their time. One of the state nurse surveyors who I knew well from having worked with her at the mothership hospital called me that afternoon and told me that with my years of experience, she was surprised that we had called them to come and inspect the hospital when we were not ready. I struggled to respond to her and tried not to tell her that the CEO did not know what he was doing and finally told her that while I had tried to have our CEO call off the visit, he had refused. I ended up apologizing for him and was angry that he had refused to listen to me and put me in this position.

The CEO had set up a hiring policy that stated that every person hired would be interviewed by him, the chief financial officer (CFO) and chief nurse, and they would have to be approved by all three before the person would be hired. On one particular occasion, I did not sign off on a potential hire. He happened to be a friend of the CEO's son who worked as a sous chef in the kitchen. The son complained to his father that I did not sign off on his friend. The CEO then sent out an email to all staff informing us that he had known this applicant for three years and that he would be a good employee and would be hired. Frustrated, I told him if he was not going to listen to my recommendation then why should I waste my time interviewing employees who were not going to report to me? He did not answer me. The individual was hired, but on the first day of employment, while in orientation, he had to be pulled from class because he had failed the drug test. The HR director called me and asked me how I knew not to hire him. My response was that when you have been in the business as long as I had, it was not hard to identify people who were on drugs. The CEO never said anything to me, and we never discussed the situation.

After two years of working with him, I was getting ready to call the corporate CEO and ask to be reassigned as I could not take the stress any longer. At almost the same time, I was asked by the corporate CEO to have lunch with him. He asked me if I was ready to take over the position of CEO of the Heart Hospital as he had decided that he needed to make a change. I respectfully asked him not to do that to me as the doctors would think that I had asked that the CEO be fired so I could have his job. I asked him to just leave me in my present position and appoint someone else as the new CEO. A new CEO was appointed after he fired the current CEO. The CEO would not leave the premises when he was fired as he thought that the doctors would protect him and he could not be fired, but he forgot that the corporation had a 51 percent ownership and the doctors only had a 49 percent ownership.

The physician owners were not happy with this decision and so they decided to boycott the hospital and cancelled all of their cases. I was asked by one of the doctors if I had told the corporate CEO that the Heart Hospital CEO did not know operations, and my response was, "Yes." When he asked me why, I responded that no one person was bigger than the entire hospital.

Due to the fact that we were a new hospital and our census was just beginning to grow, the staff were very afraid that the hospital might close and they would all lose their jobs. We had a meeting with the staff, and I told them that the doctors would come back; they were just angry and trying to make a statement. When they asked, "What shall we do in the meantime?" I suggested to them that they catch up on all of the paperwork that needed to be completed while there was a lull in the action.

Two weeks later, when they realized why the CEO had been fired, the doctors placed all of their cases back on the schedule, and it was business as usual. One of the cardiologists came into the catheterization lab singing the song, "The Boys Are Back in Town." Things were back to normal.

CHAPTER 22

Leaving the Hospital Safety Net

Three years after opening the hospital, I decided it was time to leave. A vascular surgeon came into my office complaining that he just could not understand why we told a doctor we could not do his heart case when we were trying to build the business. He did not seem to understand that if we did not have an open-heart nurse to recover the patient, the case could not be done. After that conversation, I had had enough of hospital work and being yelled at by doctors because I did not have enough nurses. I guess they thought that I had a machine that I could just turn the handle and crank out more nurses. I told myself that was enough trying to please doctors; my days of being yelled at by physicians were over. And after thirty-seven years of working in a hospital, I had enough, and it was time to leave the hospital environment. The enjoyment of working in a hospital was over, and I wanted a new experience. I had worked for the corporation for thirty-seven years, and I was no longer enjoying my job; it was time to leave. It was a scary situation leaving the hospital setting which I had known my entire career, but it is important to know when to leave, so you take a risk and move on; this is how we grow. Remembering that I had a letter in my safety deposit box that stated that I could get a year's severance pay along with benefits, I asked to be laid off, and the CEO reluctantly agreed to do so.

Shortly before my decision to leave, the corporate CEO had himself been relieved of his position and a new corporate CEO was hired. When the new corporate CEO learned of my severance package, he told my boss that I was not entitled to one year's severance pay. My boss told him about my letter, and he asked to see it. So I went to my safety deposit box and provided the requested letter as proof. The hospital attorney then drafted my severance package document which I had to sign, prohibiting me from working for the competing hospital for a period of one year. Signing that letter felt very good, and I then proceeded to ask the corporate attorney about my ability to apply for unemployment pay. He quickly told me that I was not eligible. Asking no other questions, my employment with Community Medical Centers was over.

Before leaving this job, a job offer by a local private community college to teach in the LVN-to-RN nursing program was presented to me. I needed the change and loved teaching, so my answer was that I would seriously think about it after taking the summer off. Taking an entire summer off was something that had not been possible in the past. I took the entire summer off to travel with my husband and do some of the things on my bucket list. We flew to Denver and then drove to South Dakota to see Mount Rushmore; we flew to Mexico twice, once to Leon and once to Guadalajara to listen and sing with Mariachis. We visited our son and family in San Diego and just took time to relax and enjoy each other. That was a great summer.

My husband belonged to the Knights of Columbus, and one night at one of his meetings, my friend who was also a Knight and had been the DJ at our wedding, asked my husband about me. He informed him that I had just been laid off. My friend who just happened to work for the California Employment Development Department (EDD) asked him if I had applied for unemployment insurance pay, and my husband told him that I had been informed by the hospital attorney that I was not eligible. He told my husband to have me call him that night. When I called him and told him what I had been told about not being eligible, he said to me, "Of course, you are eligible!" and asked me to get on the computer and apply. My application was submitted that night, and it was approved. Upon receiving my first check, I immediately went to the Coach store and bought my first Coach purse. Somewhere along the line, my belief is that the hospital tried to have my unemployment insurance payments and payments actually were stopped. When I questioned this action with the Unemployment Department, I was asked to send them a copy of my severance letter. Upon their review of the letter, they found that the wording was such that it did allow me to receive unemployment payments so I continued to receive unemployment pay along with my severance pay until I accepted the new job in October.

Wondering whether there would be life outside of the hospital world would be a new adventure. One of my personal policies that I had always used was to never look back on a decision. Once a decision is made, then just move forward and don't dwell on the past. Upon leaving Community Hospital, I realized how much my husband's death had impacted my mental health while still working at the hospital where he died. Every time I walked by the hospital room where he had been a patient, or walked down the hallway from the catheterization lab to ICU where he had traveled on a gurney, I was impacted. When walking by the ICU room where he eventually was taken off life support and died, I was affected but would dismiss the feelings as I was still employed at the facility. When I finally left, all of these feelings came front and center, and I realized how deep an impact his death at this hospital had left on me.

I taught for one year and then accepted a position as a project manager working on a grant that had been given to the Hospital Council of Northern and Central California. Governor Schwarzenegger had given the Central Valley a grant of almost $500,000 to implement four projects in the Central Valley for nursing. First, we were to increase the number of nurses for the Central Valley.

Second, we were to train more nursing faculty in order to be able to increase the number of nursing students. Third, we were to implement a computerized clinical placement system for clinical placement for nursing students. The last piece of the grant was to help with distance education. Working with nurse leaders in both academia and service in the Central Valley, we were able to accomplish all the requirements of the grant. We added over 400 nurses, trained sixty-four additional nursing faculty, implemented a computerized clinical placement system that is still in place today, and provided distance nursing education for the south valley. With the completion of the grant, I was free to look for other employment.

The California Institute for Nursing and Health Care (CINHC) was seeking to hire a diversity director for the state of California responsible for increasing the diversity of the nursing workforce in California. I was interested in their mission and traveled to the Los Angeles area to interview for this position. There were three people who interviewed and I was offered the position, so taking another risk, I joined CINHC. The position was being funded by a grant for two years, so it was made clear to me that if more funding could not be located, the job would have to end. CINHC was based in Berkeley, but I was allowed to remain in the valley and would commute on the train to Berkeley every month for meetings with the CINHC team. CINHC was led by a dynamic nurse leader, former chief nurse at Kaiser and a well-respected nurse leader in California, Delores J. I reported to Bob P., the assistant administrator and a fun person to work with, and supervised a very dedicated nurse who was as passionate as me about increasing the number of minority nurses in health care, Josie C. Josie was a dynamic recruiter with students, and they loved her. Many a minority student was encouraged and sought a nursing career because of Josie. Together, we developed a list of minority nursing organizations in California and reached out to minority students and encouraged them to seek a career in nursing. We developed a CD titled, "Breaking the Barriers," which interviewed minority nurses and nursing students across the state who shared the barriers and challenges that they had overcome in order to reach their goal of becoming a registered nurse. The purpose of this CD was to show minority students that if other students like themselves had made it and reached their goals, they could too. This CD is being used in different nursing programs across the nation to encourage minority students to keep their goal of becoming a nurse and overcome the many barriers that they might face.

At the completion of the two years, I left CINHC to work on another grant with the Hospital Council of Northern and Central California to develop a medical respite unit. This was a new challenge for me as I had never worked on this type of program before.

I was fortunate to work with some dynamic healthcare leaders in the Central Valley including Lynne A., who was the regional vice president for the Hospital Council and had applied for the original grant with Kaiser Permanente. We were able to open an eight-bed medical respite unit at the Fresno Rescue Mission with a grant supported by Kaiser Permanente. It served as a medical respite unit for the homeless who were discharged from the hospital but still needed follow-up care to keep them from having to be readmitted to the hospital. I had the opportunity to help furnish a designated area of the Mission in order to provide a place where the homeless could receive post-hospital care other than out in the streets. St. Agnes Hospital provided eight hospital beds and Kaiser and Community Hospitals along with St. Agnes each provided monies to help support the new venture in hopes of decreasing the readmission of homeless patients to the hospitals. Sierra Vista Clinic provided the nurse who followed the patients at the respite unit. The program was successful, has expanded its capacity, and is still in existence today. This job helped me gain more knowledge about the needs of the homeless and how best to help them with their medical care.

CHAPTER 23

Moving to Academia

In 2011, a nurse colleague of mine who lived in San Diego knew that one of my sons lived in the area and that I had talked about wanting to move there. So when one of the private universities in the area was looking for a director for their failing nursing program, she called me and asked if she could submit my name to the provost of the school who also happened to be the co-owner of the private university. I was not really sure if this was a good idea, but again, was willing to take a risk and told her that she could give her my name. She told me that they were willing to pay up to $150,000 for the position. My thinking was that the California Board of Registered Nursing (BRN) would never approve me to serve as the nursing director as I did not have any experience as an assistant director at a nursing school. I had met the provost on a previous visit to the school to speak with her about CINHC's diversity program since this school primarily served minority students so she remembered me from that meeting. She called and interviewed me over the phone and told me that she wanted to submit my name to the BRN for approval. I shared my concerns with her about being approved but gave her permission to submit my name. I went about my business knowing that the approval would probably never come. To my surprise, she called me back the day before the Fourth of July and told me that I had been approved by the Board. I was shocked! Now what? I was excited and scared at the same time as I said yes to her offer. When asking about the pay, she offered me $120,000, and I again took a risk and told her this was not enough money to get me to move all the way to the San Diego area, and so we settled on $140,000. She needed me to begin as soon as possible so we agreed on a start date of the last week in August.

After hanging up the phone I let my husband know what had happened, and we began to make plans to move. We did not want to take the time to sell our home so decided to rent it. Now we would have to try to find a home in the Chula Vista area, find a mover, and start packing. We found a one-story house in Chula Vista near where the university was located and worked with a management company to rent our home. Since my efforts to move to San Diego after my husband had died had not materialized, I asked God for help and told Him that if he wanted us to move, then He had to make it happen; I was putting it in His hands. This time everything seemed to fall into place. We had to have three-yard sales in order to sell all the items we were not going to take with us, and made plans for the move. This went on for weeks until we had emptied the house. I began packing right away. I was working full-time, so I would come home every night and I needed to pack one section of the house before I could go to bed; the next day, it was back to work. We made arrangements with a moving company to move all of our furniture, and the management company found a renter for our home. I was worried about renting my home as once before, my first husband and I had a rental home, and it was nothing but problems, but the renters seemed very nice so that eased our minds somewhat.

The next job was to find a home in Chula Vista, the town where the university was located. We wanted a one-story home as it was hard for both of us to climb stairs, and we were finally able to find one that we liked that was single story. There were six people ahead of us who wanted to rent this house so our chances did not look good. However, after proving my starting salary to the management company who was renting the home, we suddenly moved to the top of the list and moved in one week before I was to begin my new job. It was not just about packing our things, but once we were in our new home, we now had to unpack everything and get used to living in our new home and learn how to negotiate the different freeways and learn our way around the area. My son, daughter-in-law, and granddaughter who lived in the area were able to help us unpack. They were happy to have us closer, but our other son and family who lived in the Central Valley were sad to see us leave. My brother and his wife at the time also lived in the area, so it was nice to be able to spend more time with them.

I was both excited and scared to begin my new job; another risk-taking. Having worked in hospitals most of my life, this was a new arena for me. My only experience in academia was the small amount of time spent teaching licensed vocational nurses to become registered nurses. There was a huge learning curve ahead of me and prayer was in order. The provost had told me that she would be available to help me, but just before starting the job, she was diagnosed with pancreatic cancer and had to undergo treatment, so she was not as available as I needed other than on the phone. Thank goodness for one of the other deans, Dr. M., who took me under her wing and helped me. I worked long hours to try to learn what was needed, and after a few days, this dean said to me, "Boy, you really work."

When I asked her what she meant by that comment, she informed me that the previous director who had preceded me would come in at nine thirty in the morning, would sit around and drink coffee until eleven thirty when it was time to go to lunch and then would spend two to three hours at lunch, come back and work a couple of hours, and then it was time to go home. No wonder the school was in trouble; people were not doing their job. When she learned that the BRN was coming for a visit, she quit the day before they arrived and left the school and the assistant director in a huge bind.

There was a lot to learn and I had to learn fast. The school was on the verge of being shut down by the California BRN due to many deficiencies which had not been corrected, and it had a bad reputation in the area with the other nursing programs. Before moving there to take on the role of director, I was called by the BRN's Nurse Education Consultant for the school on the orders of the executive director of the Board of Registered Nursing to make sure that I was aware of all the problems with the school. I was also told by one of the nursing directors in the San Diego Consortium, "You know that you have a great reputation in the state; you must know that, so why are you putting your reputation at risk by taking the director role at this school?" I responded that I was not worried about my reputation and that I wanted to try to help this school and the nursing students succeed. It is not always about taking the easy road; it is about taking a risk and making a difference. Regardless of the problems, I was not going to back out now. Some of my nursing colleagues across the state wondered why I was taking on this challenge and tried to talk me out of taking the job. But I felt sorry for the students, mainly minority students, and felt someone had to step up to the plate to try to help the school stay open so that one hundred plus nursing students would be able to graduate. I knew that I was taking on a big challenge, but have always loved challenges, so for me it was, "Damn the torpedoes, full speed ahead."

Because the students were scared and did not have a leader in place as the director of nursing had left the day before the BRN arrived for their visit, there was much anxiety amongst the students about being able to finish their program so they were calling the BRN on a daily basis to complain about not receiving any communication from the leaders of the school. So even before moving to Chula Vista, I established a communication system for the students to try to keep them informed. I implemented what was called the "1500 Newscast" in which an email was sent out to all students every Tuesday and Friday at 3:00 p.m. to provide them with information about what was happening at the school. My first day of work I had a meeting with all of the students to try to calm their fears. I began the process of hiring full-time staff as previously, the nursing program had only used *per diem* or part-time instructors. While I had a big learning curve as I had never run a nursing program before, I had years and years of management experience to help me. It took all of my management experience to make a difference. There was a total of three cohorts of entry-level master students as well as several cohorts of family nurse practitioner students enrolled in the School of Nursing; I met with all of the faculty and shared my expectations as well as with the students and promised that I would do everything in my power to get them through the program. This seemed to calm their fears and the calls to the BRN stopped.

I remember being asked by the Nursing Education Consultant to put together a report on our progress so that she could submit it to the Board for their next meeting. I wrote up the report the way I thought she would want it and left to go to the airport to catch my flight back to Fresno. Before moving, I had made a commitment to do a presentation in Hanford the next day, so I was going to fly back to Fresno, stay with my friend Carolyn that night, get up the next morning, do the presentation, and then fly back to San Diego that evening. While I was sitting in the airport awaiting my flight, I was called by the Nursing Education Consultant to whom I had submitted my report and was reamed up one side and down the other telling how bad my report was that I had submitted. She told me that I needed to redo the report with more specific information and that she needed to have it by nine o'clock the next morning. Wondering how I would ever get it redone, I knew there was no choice. After arriving at my friend's home and eating dinner, I asked to use her computer. Starting to work on the report at 9:00 p.m. it was not completed until three o'clock the next morning. I still needed to take a quick shower, go to bed, and sleep for two hours before getting up at 6:00 a.m. in order to be in Hanford by

8:00 a.m. I did my presentation, drove back to Fresno to catch my plane, and slept all the way back to San Diego. This should have been a clue to me as to how hard I was going to have to work in order to help this school.

One of my jobs as the director was to find clinical placements at the local facilities for the nursing students to complete their required clinical rotation and hours. This was not easy due to the reputation of the school. I learned that prior to my arrival, records had been altered by the nursing administration that indicated that one of the previous cohorts had completed their pediatric rotation when, in fact, that was not true. The school did not have all of the required BRN approved staff, the passing score on the national exam was below 75 percent which is a requirement of the BRN, the school did not have enough faculty, policies were not in place, etc. I began the process of making the necessary changes to correct the deficiencies.

Almost every month my presence was required before the BRN to answer questions about the progress we were making. The meetings were very stressful, and at every meeting, there was a threat to close our program down, but we worked very hard to convince the Board to give us more time to meet all of the requirements. At every meeting, I was made to feel defeated. We were trying so hard to correct the problems, and while being told by the Board that they appreciated my hard work, they were still mad at the school. I remember praying to God to help me and telling Him, "I know you did not send me to Chula Vista to fail; please help me save this nursing program."

Sometimes, after a very stressful meeting, all I could do was go home and cry and then return the next day to work on correcting the problems. Lucky for me, I had some wonderful faculty that worked with me who were very supportive, and it was through all our hard work that we were able to save the nursing program.

At every meeting, there was a public member who would come to the meeting on her scooter, and she would always go up to the front of the room which was disruptive. As the Board was questioning me and making their remarks, she would prance back and forth across the room, putting her finger across her neck in an action in which she was telling the board to cut off our head; in other words, to shut our program down. The fact that the Board members did nothing to stop her behavior or tell her to take her seat and be respectful made it even harder for our school as other public members seemed to agree with her. I named her "Frenchie" and dreaded to see her roll her scooter into the room. She was very distracting as she would keep getting in and out of her scooter.

I would have to sit in front of the Board sometimes for an hour and a half, answering questions. When they finally finished asking their questions, I felt like I had been run over by a Mack truck. It was a horrible experience, one that left me scarred and hurt by the way I was treated. The BRN was being sun downed by the governor at the end of December of that year. They desperately tried to schedule a meeting of the Board before the end of the year to discuss our school and try to shut it down, but they were not able to get a quorum for the meeting, thus they were not able to take any action. I felt God's response to my prayers.

As I stated earlier, one of my jobs was to find the clinical placement for students. There was a person who had been hired as a clinical placement coordinator, and when we kept asking her if she had found the clinical placements at certain facilities, she would lie to us and tell us we had the placements only to find out that this was not true. When she failed to report to work one day, and we were told that she was in her car crying and could no longer continue in the job, we realized that we did not have the clinical placements that she had told us we had, and we had to scramble to find the placements for the students. Since the school was not nationally certified, the only hospital we could take our students for their pediatric clinical experience was Navy Balboa Hospital. Due to the fact that not all hospitals have pediatric units anymore, it is a real challenge to get pediatric clinical placements. The person who did the scheduling for the hospital was a person who liked to make sure that you knew that she had the power. If she was not happy with you, she would yell and lecture you and seemed to take joy in letting you know what you had done wrong. One day after being yelled at by her, I kept my cool and informed her that as an adult one did not appreciate being yelled at or lectured to and that if she had a problem with something, that it would be appreciated it if she would let me know and I would do everything in my power to fix the problem. It must have been the wrong thing to say as that evening, my phone dinged off the hook as she cancelled all of our pediatric clinical placements at Navy Balboa Hospital which had already been approved. That put us in a real bind as pediatrics was the next rotation, and if we did not have clinical placements, the BRN would have another reason why they should shut us down.

This action totally stressed me out, and we wondered how we would be able to provide the pediatric experience that our students needed. Knowing that the other nursing directors in the area would not be willing nor anxious to help as they wanted our nursing program to be closed, I had to think out of the box. Being a member of the Association of California Nurse Leaders (ACNL), my search for pediatric placements began by using my networking abilities to try to find an alternate location. Our COO told me not to worry, that he had a friend who was the CEO at a hospital in Las Vegas, and he was sure he would let us bring our students to his hospital for their pediatric experience. I informed him that the BRN would never approve this as it was not a California facility. Since pediatric clinical spots are very hard to come by, many calls were made to colleagues across the state with no success. Finally, I called the director of the Shriners Hospital of Northern California in Stockton, BJ, and asked her whether we could bring our students to her hospital after explaining what had happened. She was kind enough to say yes; in fact, she said, "For you, Pilar, anything." I was thrilled having found a location, but now we had to work on the logistics of this plan. I met with our nursing faculty who was very supportive and wanted our students to succeed.

The first step to make this happen was to speak with our pediatric instructor and ask her if she and her husband would be willing to move to Stockton and stay in a hotel for one month so we could send our students to Shriners. We offered to pay for her travel expenses, and their room and board. She and her husband agreed.

Next, we had to divide the cohort into four groups and worked with the chief operating officer who used his personal credit card to make flight and hotel reservations for all of the students. Each of the four groups went up to Stockton for a week at a time and completed their clinical rotation doing twelve-hour shifts and supplemented the hours with simulation. The students received a great clinical experience at Shriners Hospital caring for their pediatric patients and felt that their pediatric experience had been enhanced caring for the patients at Shriners Hospital. They came back excited about their experience and enthusiastic about pediatric nursing. At the completion of the month, we all breathed a sigh of relief as all the students had completed their pediatric hours in full.

Feeling like this had been an injustice for our students, I wrote a letter to the captain, the chief nurse at the Navy Hospital explaining to her what had happened. Not being able to speak with her prior to having to send the students to Stockton, she was informed of what had happened and reminded her that many of our students were veterans and had a right to do their pediatric clinical rotation at Navy Balboa Hospital. She agreed. The person who had cancelled all of our placements was reassigned to another position. After this happened, I was contacted by a couple of the other nursing directors in the area and was told, "We have been trying to get rid of her for years; how did you manage do it in just a few months?" My response was that I did not put up with any disrespectful behavior.

All of the three cohorts of students who were registered at the school on my arrival were able to graduate. My job was done, and I felt very good about this accomplishment. My desire to retire again reemerged so having given notice to the president of United States University, a search was started for a new director. My husband asked me if we were going to stay in Chula Vista or return home. My response to him was that I was a valley girl and wanted to go back home. My employment with the university ended in mid-June when a new dean of the nursing school was brought onboard. The president of the university told me that he was going to recommend me to become a member of the University Board of Trustees, and I was appointed to that position the following year.

CHAPTER 24

Coming Home

We had rented our house, and the management company had found our latest renter. While she started out paying the rent on time, after a few months, she fell behind and then stopped paying it all together. Her in-laws who had moved in with her and her husband had left, and shortly after they left, her husband moved out and she was left on her own to pay the rent. She found new renters to move into the house which were not approved and even had people living in the garage. To save money, she stopped watering the grass, plants, and trees, and since it was a very hot summer, everything started to die. The house looked like it was in foreclosure when we were finally made aware of the situation. We came home to check things out and to let her know ourselves that we were moving back and needed her to be out of the house. She did not want to leave, but she was already five months late with her rent, and we needed our home. When we came to check things out, we began to water the trees, flowers, and grass, and she was very upset because we were using power that she had to pay. She tried telling me that we were going to get in trouble as it was not a watering day, to which I responded, "Since when do they have watering days in the county?" Unable to get me to stop watering, she then sent out her pit bull dog, who was really just a pup and took off running when I scared it away. I continued my watering, and she then called the sheriff's on us and complained that we were trespassing. When the sheriff arrived and asked me what we were doing, my response was that we were simply taking care of our property. I soon realized that renters seemed to have more rights than property owners. It was difficult to get her out of the house, but she finally did move taking with her my microwave, dishwasher cutlery container, and other items.

One of the items we had left behind when we moved to Chula Vista was my mother's antique porch swing. She tried to sell it to my sister who had stopped by at her yard sale. She did not know she was my sister and proceeded to tell her that she and her family had made the swing. Luckily, my sister called me right away and we were able to stop her from selling it. I guess you will do almost anything when you need money. She tried to tell me that she was actually selling a child's swing. I told her she was lying as my sister certainly would know the difference between my mother's swing and a child's swing. The swing was saved. My husband had also left a trailer at the home, and she told a friend that he could take it as my husband had died and would not need it. After we returned to our home, we had to search for the trailer and luckily found it not too far from our house. We called the sheriff and told him of the situation. He went with us to the house where we had seen the trailer which was now filled with trash, and we were able to retrieve it. The sheriff told us that a bunch of thieves lived in the house where we had found our trailer. We brought our trailer home, trash and all.

We returned home almost two years after we had left for Chula Vista. I remember being back for two days when I saw a tractor pulling a trailer across an intersection and I thought, *We are home!*

Before leaving United States University, I was called by a friend at Fresno State, and she told me that she heard I was moving back and wanted to know if I was interested in working at Fresno State. I told her that I might be interested in part-time work but not a fulltime job. The position was the director of the Central California Center for Excellence in Nursing. I was interviewed by the dean of the College of Health and Human Services and was offered a parttime position even though the job called for a full-time person. My primary job was to work with the nursing faculty on research projects and find grants for the School of Nursing, which I was able to work with a team to secure over 2 million dollars in grant funding. One of the grants was to fund a mobile health unit to provide screenings for diabetes, blood pressure, and cholesterol for people in rural areas. The Bachelor of Nursing Students and family nurse practitioner students, with their faculty, manned the unit. This has been a very popular program that is still being utilized today. I worked with the nursing faculty and helped them apply for grants for their program. I enjoyed working with them and worked closely with the dean to implement and complete various programs.

CHAPTER 25

Tragedy Strikes Again

My husband Felix and I had been married for thirteen years. We married in 2002 and enjoyed extensive traveling, going to the movies, visiting with our sons and grandchildren. He taught me how to enjoy tequila and baseball. Felix loved his grandchildren, and they loved him; they called him Papa and he spoiled them. He also would spoil me, calling me his queen, making dinner for us every evening so that I would not have to cook after working all day. He made me my cup of coffee in the mornings and even pulled out my car out of the garage for me in the morning; I could just drive forward and go to work. We enjoyed spending time with his sisters and family and enjoyed our vacations in Mexico in our timeshare at Cabo San Lucas. As he was born in Mexico, he was like a different person in his own country and became my personal tour guide as we visited many different cities in that beautiful country.

Shortly after our marriage, he began to have cardiac symptoms of shortness of breath, indigestion, and tiredness when exerting himself. After much prodding, he finally sought medical care and was referred to a cardiologist. His EKG showed changes during his stress test, and he was scheduled for a cardiac catheterization the next day. He was only in the catheterization lab for a short while when his cardiologist came out and told me he had a severe blockage in his main coronary artery and needed to have open-heart surgery the next day as the blockage was too high to place a stent in the area.

The next morning, he underwent open-heart surgery, and as they wheeled him away, I remember telling him, "Don't you dare die on me, Felix." He was slow to awaken after the surgery and was in the hospital for five days and recovered at home. His longstanding high blood pressure, however, had taken a toll on his heart, and he developed congestive heart failure and was treated with medication for the first few years. Eventually because the ejection fraction of his heart was very low, he had a pacemaker/defibrillator placed in his chest and was followed closely by his cardiologist. Life was good again, and we enjoyed many days together.

On June 6th, 2015, our son, daughter-in-law, her nephew, and our grandchildren had come over to visit. The next morning, we had breakfast, and because it was a warm day, the grandkids wanted to go swimming and convinced Felix to go out to the pool with them. He was playing with them while I was in the house cleaning up the breakfast dishes, and my son had gone into town to buy some toys to use in the pool. My daughter-in-law came into the house and told me that something had happened to Felix. He had dived into the pool and had not surfaced. I ran out and helped pull him out of the pool. I immediately went into my nurse mode doing CPR as my daughter-in-law, Alisha, called 911. He was unresponsive, and the CPR was continued until the paramedics arrived. I could hear the siren in the distance and a helicopter flew above. The paramedics defibrillated his heart, but there was no response. They put him in an ambulance and took him to the hospital, doing CPR the entire time. I rushed into the house to change, and my son was called back by his wife, and he drove me to the hospital. Knowing that Felix had a bad heart, I was not confident that he would survive this event, and he did not. He died on June 7, 2015, surrounded by my son, myself, his daughter, and his brother and his sisters.

Having lost my first husband, I knew what to expect with regards to making funeral arrangements. My family all came to be with me, and my friends were all very supportive. I was comforted by the fact that he had not suffered a long painful death, but the shock of losing him was very hard. I lost my first husband on June 5 and my second husband on June 7; consequently, I do not like the month of June. In fact, the last week of May, I begin to feel down, sad and somewhat depressed and this lasts until after June 7; it happens every year, and thus I plan to be extra nice to myself during this time, and my family knows that I need support during this time of the year and provide it via phone calls and cards.

Felix wanted to be cremated, and so we made the arrangements with the funeral home. We had a rosary in the evening and the Mass of Christian burial the next morning. My son, Jeff, delivered the eulogy, and both of our granddaughters also spoke, having written their own words that they wanted to share about their Papa; it was very touching. The church was full with friends and family, and we had a nice reception at one of Felix's favorite Mexican restaurants after the service. Again, my family and friends helped me get through this loss, and I was comforted by all their cards and kind words. I could tell that Felix was really loved by the people that knew him. His son, who had not talked with him for a long time, came to give his condolences, and I wondered why he had not been able to come and visit his own father while he was still alive. Now, it was too late.

As my family and friends left, once again I was alone. Never questioning God as to why me a second time. I recognized the fact that God must have wanted him to come home, and it was not up to me to question why. I have often said that if you lose a parent, you share that experience with your siblings and support one another. If you lose a child, as hard as it is, you share that experience with your spouse and try as best you can to comfort one another. But when you lose a spouse, you walk that road alone as no one else knows what it was like being married to that person. I was now walking it for a second time, and the sun was still coming up every morning and life was moving on without stopping. My job was to also keep going.

Since I had made it through once before, I knew that I could make it through this time; there was no other choice. I took one month off from work to take care of all the notifications that had to take place and close accounts. When the month was over, I was happy to return to work in order to keep my mind off of the loss. I missed my coffee and paper in the morning and my car being turned around; I missed his humor and his voice, but knew that he had joined Joe in looking out for me up in heaven. Somehow, that helped to ease my pain and sorrow.

I remember telling my sister Mattie that I would never marry again; twice was enough, and I did not want to go through this heartache a third time, but she told me that she was sure that I would find love again. I emphatically disagreed. I engulfed myself in my work at Fresno State as I made plans to live as a single one more time. I would see couples holding hands as they walked together and I would cry, realizing how much I missed Felix. My granddaughter Gracie would start to cry anytime someone mentioned his name, and it took her over a year to get over the loss as she was very close to him. He had given her a big Mickey Mouse doll, and she carried that doll around with her wherever she went for almost a year; she still sleeps with it. Almost one year after his death, his family, my son and his family, and I got together and spread his ashes. While he was no longer alive, we knew that he would always be with us in our hearts.

CHAPTER 26

Recovering a Second Time

Prior to Felix's death, I had been contacted by a nurse colleague and asked whether I would be interested in applying to serve on the California Board of Registered Nursing. Having discussed this decision with Felix, who was always very supportive and proud of my efforts and accomplishments, he encouraged me to apply. After giving it much thought, my application was sent to the governor of California for consideration. I thought it was ironic that in the past, I had been a regular person coming before the Board to defend my school, and now, my application was being reviewed for a possible appointment to the California Board of Registered Nursing. Along with my application, five letters of recommendations from healthcare leaders were submitted. I was encouraged to seek letters of support from the Hispanic Women's Caucus and other minority organizations in the state. However, since I did not know anyone on those committees, I did not do so and felt that if I could not earn the position on my own merits, then I probably did not deserve to be selected to serve. This process began in April of 2015, and it was a long waiting period due to the vetting process. After months of waiting and wondering whether I was still being considered, I received confirmation by the Governor's office that not only was I still in the vetting process but was the number one candidate for the position. In October 2015, while in San Diego for a United States University Board of Trustees meeting, I received a call from Governor Brown's office, letting me know that I had been appointed to the Board for a four-year term. I had come full circle. I felt that this appointment was the pinnacle of my nursing career. My only regret was that Felix had died before I was appointed to the Board; he would have been so proud. I knew that he was cheering for me from up in heaven. I attended my first meeting as a Board member in January 2016 and completed my term on June 1, 2019.

I considered it an honor to have served my profession and was proud of my service. This appointment kept me very busy as there were meetings out of town every month except for the months of July and December when the Board did not meet. The majority of the work involved reviewing cases before each meeting—the cases were of nurses who had either lost their license or been placed on probation and were now seeking reinstatement. Inundated with BRN material to review, I decided not to seek a second term. One of my goals when I was appointed to the BRN was to have the Board come to Fresno and hold a meeting in the Central Valley. When I first approached the other Board members about meeting in Fresno, they were reluctant, but I told them that I would not give up until a meeting was held in Fresno. Happy to report that the Board met in Fresno not just once during my four-year term, but twice, and the nursing students were very appreciative of having the opportunity to see the Board in action in their own backyard.

While working for Fresno State, I had the opportunity to travel to Cuba with a group of California nursing leaders. I was the only one from the Central San Joaquin Valley to be part of the group. There were also two people from the Stockton area who joined this group. We were able to visit hospitals, clinics, and nursing schools in Cuba and learn about how health care is delivered in this country. I was impressed with how they delivered care, especially their home visits by doctors and nurses who were responsible for maintaining the health of their local community. It was a great opportunity to learn about Cuba, see the beautiful old cars that had been maintained and now used as taxis, eat the good food, and drink the mojitos. I will always remember this trip as one of the highlights of my career.

After working for Fresno State for four years, my desire to finally retire surfaced and I gave my resignation letter to the dean.

She did not want me to leave and asked me to stay, but my mind was made up. Soon after that, I was contacted by a nurse colleague, Roxanna S, a faith community nurse who told me that the bishop and monsignor wanted to know when I was going to retire. When I asked her why, she told me that the diocese had a grant they wanted me to work on for them. Before making a decision whether to accept or decline the offer, I consented to speak with the monsignor who gave me the information about the grant. I debated as to whether I wanted to take this on, but as I thought about it, I told myself that I had done a lot for my profession but questioned what I had done for my church other than sing in the choir. So I decided to accept the offer to work on the two-year grant to provide health services and education to Hispanics in the rural areas of the of the diocese which runs from Merced to Bakersfield and includes Tehachapi.

So having failed retirement three times now, I began my work with the diocese and developed an outreach plan to visit all of the nine vicariates in the Diocese of Fresno. I would call and ask the head of each vicariate to speak to his priests at one of his vicariate meetings. We would be invited to present information on the survey process in hopes that we would be invited to survey the Hispanic parishioners of at least one parish in the vicariate. One of the churches in the Fresno Vicariate had developed a health survey in English that had been approved by the diocese, and we had it translated into Spanish. Once a parish was identified, we would attend the Mass and present information on the survey and ask the adult parishioners to complete the survey and turn it in to us at the end of the service. We found that we received the best response when the parish priest would encourage them to complete the survey and stress the importance of gaining the information contained in the survey.

BUT I WANT TO BE A NURSE

Once the surveys were collected, they were tabulated with all of the information contained in the survey and graphs were developed for each parish where the survey was distributed. The priest could then view the educational needs of his Hispanic parishioners, and education on the subjects of need could be developed and presented to the Hispanic parishioners. Before starting to distribute any of the Spanish surveys, we had a hypothesis that considering diabetes and heart disease was high among Hispanics, these two topics would be of great interest to the Hispanic parishioners. Our hypothesis proved to be true, but we were surprised to find out how many Hispanics also wanted information on stress management. Because I had worked with Fresno State School of Nursing to obtain the original grant for the mobile health unit, I was able to make arrangements to bring the mobile health unit to rural churches and use the services to screen parishioners. We had first used it at a convocation of priests held in Visalia. The priests were a little hesitant and nervous to find out their numbers with regards to blood pressure, cholesterol, and blood glucose, but the bishop led the group, and with a little prodding, the priests followed. It was interesting to see their reaction after undergoing the screening. They were like little kids so happy with their results and wanting to share them with their fellow priests and the nurses.

The rural areas were the perfect place to bring the mobile health unit. Many of the Hispanics in the rural areas do not have a primary care physician, and there are few, if any, medical facilities in the rural areas. These individuals have to travel to the larger cities in order to receive preventative care, and many do not trust the health care system in America. Bringing health care to them was important because many of them do not seek preventative health care due to not having insurance, lack of transportation and having to pay for someone to take them back and forth to the doctor, fear of deportation, being monolingual (Spanish), etc. Through the mobile health unit, patients with very high blood pressure or very high blood sugars or cholesterol are identified and then referred for follow-up either with a physician, clinic, or emergency room or urgent care. Many of these individuals had no idea that they had a very high blood sugar and had diabetes or such a high blood pressure that they were in danger of having a stroke. A diabetic educator also went out with the mobile health unit and was able to explain correct foods and portions that these individuals should be eating. It is impossible to determine how many strokes or heart attacks this mobile health unit was able to prevent, but we are confident that lives have been saved. A side benefit of the mobile health unit was that it opened the eyes of the nursing students who were able to see the health care needs of minority people in the rural areas and turned them on to community health nursing. In addition to the screenings, the student nurses were able to give flu shots that were provided by the county health department. The people who took advantage of the services of the mobile unit were very appreciative of the services and information received. I had thought that my work with the diocese would end after the two years of the grant funding ended and that I could retire for a fourth time. Alas, the bishop decided that the diocese needed to have health ministry as a service, so my work continues, serving those less fortunate to help them gain a better knowledge of their health.

My sister Mattie was correct in her prediction. I was lucky to find love for a third time having met my third husband through Felix. When Felix and I married, a cocky young man was doing the disking on my property. I was happy just to have all the weeds cut down, but Felix was always complaining about the poor job that the young man would do. After being tired of hearing him complain, I told him that if he was not happy with the young man's work that he should find someone else to do the disking, and he did. He found David Samoulian. David owned his own business, David's Custom Tractor Work, and has all the big honking equipment. I had to admit that David did a much better job with the disking. Not knowing him at first, my job was just to write the check to pay him for his services. I was not aware that David and Felix had developed a good friendship until after Felix died. Apparently, after David had finished disking, Felix would bring out his bottle of tequila and would pour David a drink, and they would sit and chat. When Felix died, David called me and asked if he could come over and give me his condolences and I said yes. A few days later, while my son Jeff and his family were here, he came over, and we had a nice conversation. I did not realize at the time that his father had just recently died. Before leaving, he told me that the next time I needed to have my property disked, that it was on him. I thought this was a very nice gesture and did call him several months later.

He would call me on the phone to check on me and told me that if I ever needed any help just call him. Once after calling him to cut down the weeds on my property, he accidently cut off a water line with his disk, and he had to shut off the power to the pump so he could fix the break. He forgot to turn the main water line back on, and upon returning home from a function that evening, there was no water. After checking the pump and trying to turn on the main faucet, there was still no water, so I called him. He told me that I had to turn the faucet very hard to the left, but it would not budge, and I did not have the strength to do it, so he came over late at night to open it up for me so that there would be water in the house. Again, a very nice gesture. I found out he has a heart of gold, is very respectful, and is always willing to help others. His good sense of humor and playfulness makes life interesting. After that event, we began to talk more often, and the rest is history. We were married on May 26, 2018, in the backyard, with family and close friends in attendance. We wanted our family to be very much involved in our ceremony and so his granddaughter, Maddie, and my granddaughters Breanna and Gracie were our junior bridesmaids, and my grandson Adrian (AJ) walked me down the aisle. My sister Esther was my matron of honor, and his good friend Jose was his best man. His son Michael and his wife, Vibha, as well as his younger son Mark, were also in attendance. Mark's wife Lara was not able to attend due to travel restrictions. We had a small wedding, with lots of good food, music, and the love of family and friends. What more could we have asked for in our marriage? I have often been told by acquaintances that some people never find love once; they want to know how I have been able to find it three times? I don't know the answer to that question but recognize how fortunate I have been to have found three men who have loved me.

CHAPTER 27
Ending a Beautiful Career

I have often said that if my career had to end tomorrow, I would say that it has been a fabulous ride! There have been no real regrets other than not joining the service. Wonderful opportunities have been placed before me, and sometimes risks were taken that helped me grow as a nurse working with some wonderful people. I have received many awards and recognition for my work and am thankful for all of them. On my graduation day in 1968, I could not have imagined that my career would have followed the path that it did. Over the past fifty-plus years of nursing, I have tried to make a small impact on the profession.

There were some wonderful mentors along my journey, and I am thankful for everything they taught me. My goal has always been to mentor other nurses who have followed in my footsteps as well as other people with whom I worked with throughout the years and tried to never forget my roots.

I remember serving as a mentor for a nursing student at Fresno City College. She called me one day and told me she was going to quit the nursing program. When I asked her why, as she was halfway through her program, she told me that she had just flunked her test, she never had time to spend with her three-year-old son, and her friends told her she was no fun anymore. Remembering what I had practiced while a student in high school by getting up really early to study, I suggested to her that she try this method. The information would be fresh in her mind, her son would be asleep so she would not be taking time away from him, and she would not be taking any away from her friends unless she called them and why would she want to do that? After doing a lot of talking, she finally agreed to give it a try. A week later, she called me, very excited, telling me that she had received a B on her test, and so she was going to stay in the program. That was great news. I lost track of her after graduation.

A couple of years later when asked to speak to a group of minority high school students at Fresno State who were interested in a health-care career, I was informed that there would be another nurse speaking to the students along with me. It was wonderful to see that she was the other nurse! It was a great feeling of satisfaction. Having been given the opportunity to speak at many events and graduations, I always encourage students to never give up on their dream; never let anyone talk you out of your dream, and share the wise words that my mother taught me, *Where there is a will, there is a way!*

I am thankful to God for allowing me to reach my dream of becoming a registered nurse. Thankful to my parents and grandparents who raised me, and all my aunts and uncles who cared about me. My brothers and sisters for loving and supporting me then and now. My husbands, Joe, Felix and David for giving me the freedom to be me, enjoy my career, and for loving me. My sons, Steve and Jeff, for being understanding and my cheerleaders and showing me their love throughout the years; my daughters-in-law, Barbara and Alisha, for being great, supportive, and loving women. I give thanks for my grandchildren, Breanna, Gracie, and Adrian (AJ) for being the greatest and so loveable. I am appreciative of my nurse colleagues and good friends for working and collaborating with me, and being my rock of Gibraltar when I most needed it; the doctors for teaching me, the students for challenging me, and all my patients for allowing me to care for them. It has indeed been a wonderful ride, and my hope is that I somehow made a difference in people's lives and in some way gave back to my profession.

I hope my words and my experiences that have been shared in this book can help someone who may be wondering whether they can overcome barriers and challenges to reach their goals. It is important for them to know that during my fifty-plus-year career, many barriers, challenges, and setbacks had to be overcome. Being human, I thought about giving up when things got tough, but I'm proud to say that I never did. I endured physical, mental, verbal, and sexual abuse, and I'm very fortunate that I never had a nervous breakdown nor had to be admitted to a mental facility and was able to work through my many issues with the help of family and friends. Facing adversity, I would always look for the positive in the situation and had a saying, "turn it around"; turn a negative into a positive and that form of thinking served me well.

I want people to know that if they put their mind to it—if they really want it—they can do anything as long as it is not illegal, immoral, or unethical. It may not be easy, but as I was often told by my father, "Nothing good ever comes easy." My hope is that through these words, I was able to reach at least one person via sharing my story; if so, then I feel that I have succeeded. I lived my life, reached my goal of becoming a registered nurse, raised two wonderful sons, and was able to do it in my own way.

About the Author

Born the oldest of six children to migrant farm workers, she began school speaking little English but was determined to excel and reach her dream of becoming a registered nurse and despite having high school counselors who were determined to have her become a secretary, she did not let anyone talk her out of her dream and proved to everyone who doubted her that determination was the key to success. Graduating from a diploma nursing program in 1968, she started her career as a staff nurse and moved up the administrative ladder to become a chief nurse executive. After obtaining her master's degree, she felt the freedom to pursue opportunities outside of the hospital setting. She is well-known throughout nursing circles across the state for her knowledge, skill, and expertise as well as her passion for helping other minority students succeed. She has been the recipient of many awards and recognitions for her work—the capstone of her successful career was being appointed to serve on the California Board of Registered Nursing by Governor Jerry Brown.

www.ingramcontent.com/pod-product-compliance
Lightning Source LLC
Chambersburg PA
CBHW031812181224
19222CB00026B/438